Contents

Acknowledgements

Another year, another Lara. Amazing. The benefit of working on a project like this—insane deadlines, mind-boggling puzzles, general dementia—is that when you work with the best people, that kind of pressure brings out the best in them. I want to thank a bunch of people, beginning with Mike Schmitt at EIDOS. Mike is the man. I'd still be somewhere near Mudubu Gorge if not for him. Kelly Zavislak and Paul Baldwin at EIDOS and the entire crew at CORE also earned high honors. Pretty much everyone at Prima Games had a big hand in this book, but Stacy DeFoe, Christy Curtis, Sara Wilson, Julie Asbury and Don Tica come immediately to mind. Finally, I'd like to dedicate this book to the big Jemaru, who lived through it. Have fun.

Introduction

Welcome back to the wonderful world of *Tomb Raider*. This release, the third installment in a classic series of *Tomb Raider* games, raises the bar another notch. We'll go right out on a very sturdy limb here: *Tomb Raider III* is the best of the bunch. This is not an easy assertion for us to make. *Tomb Raider II* was and still is an amazing game. The ambience, the thought that went into the puzzles, the architecture, and the environments—all of this makes *Tomb Raider II* head and shoulders above anything that had been done before or since. And then came *Tomb Raider III*.

It's not easy to see a true champion like *Tomb Raider II* dethroned in our hearts. But our hearts still belong to Lara, and that will have to be enough.

For the benefit of any gamers who may have stirred recently from some cave, having missed the last few years of Lara mania, perhaps some background is in order. The ongoing story of *Tomb Raider* is the story of Lara Croft—she of the privileged past and uncertain future. The daughter of Lord Henshingly Croft, Lara had lived in luxury, aloof from the world at large, until the day her plane crash-landed during a skiing holiday. Stranded and alone in the Himalayan Mountains, Lara probably should have died there, as most normal people would have. Instead, she saved herself—and in the process, transformed herself as well.

Her Himalayan odyssey was both miraculous and enlightening, as the young woman not only survived, but gained a perspective on herself and the world that made her past appear shallow and naïve. Out of the darkness of her ordeal, she saw her future reflected in a different light. She felt profoundly that there was more for her in this life than the coddled existence that had become her numbing habit. She became a seeker of truths, both large and small, and in that pursuit she continues to this day.

The story of *Tomb Raider III* begins with a meteorite that fell to earth a very long time ago and the mysterious properties that the hunk of rock displays. Over the years, pieces of the meteor have been fashioned into religious relics and scattered throughout the world. Lara becomes entangled in the quest to recover them from a variety of places around the globe. The adventure begins in India, moving through Nevada, the South Pacific Islands, and London before culminating in Antarctica.

Now, if you're just getting your feet wet in the world of Tomb Raider, the third game in the series can be a bit overwhelming. It builds a lot on what the first two games accomplished, and may assume a little much for the beginner in terms of skill level. Still, that's what we're here for. In this book resides the location of every last Secret, and every last jump in these pages has been exhaustively field-tested. Prepare yourself with a quick trip to Lara's home, and we'll get you through to the very end. And you do want to be there for the big finish. Stick with us. We know the way.

Game Basics

Tomb Raider III: Lara, CUBED

The most basic tool for guiding Lara successfully through the world of *Tomb Raider III* is an understanding of how she moves. Though each level is comprised of a variety of different types of puzzles and obstacles, the common thread is the very precise movement patterns that Lara exhibits when you manipulate the controls.

In a nutshell, Lara's world is and has always been comprised of big blocks about the same height as our heroine. The vast majority of the jumps and acrobatic feats which Lara must accomplish are directly tied to the way she moves—it's kind of like a game within a game. You have to master those nuances before you can really sit back and enjoy the big picture.

The way that Lara moves in relation to the big blocks is a constant, meaning that as long as you perform the proper move, she invariably winds up where you would intend. Of course, just when you start to feel comfortable with the basic set of jumps and flips, *Tomb Raider III* pushes the envelope in ways that even old fans may struggle with—but isn't that part of the fun?

The easiest way for newbies to get acquainted with the basics—and for old pros to familiarize themselves with the moves unique to *Tomb Raider III*—is to take a quick trip to Lara's home, where the gym and the assault course work in tandem to prepare you for the adventure ahead.

Lara's Home

A little mood music never hurt a workout.

Lara Croft's humble abode is a posh testimony to her success as a raider of tombs, and it's also a fine training ground. There's even an interesting puzzle to solve at the mansion. But first things first.

In the downstairs area, you'll find a gymnasium with some very specific workout equipment. Follow the numbers from one area to the next, and Lara will even provide narration on how to complete each task.

The gymnasium is a numbered tour through Lara's basic moves.

1: Walking to the Edge

The workout begins with a simple ledge, highlighting Lara's ability to walk to an edge without falling off. As long as you have the Walk button held down, Lara won't fall off any precipitous drop-offs, or step onto any surface which might cause her to slide out of control. Walking up to the very edge of ledges and platforms is important since that's also the way that Lara sets up for 99 percent of her jumps. It also should be noted that walking prevents Lara from being injured by such things as spikes and razor grass—not if she falls into the hazard, mind you, but walking allows her to pass through dangerous sectors of spike, plants, barbwire and the like.

Standing and jumping to grab the edge of a distant platform is another basic way in which Lara moves through her world.

Grabbing ledges is a talent that Lara employs when she can't reach a target standing up.

2: The Standing Jump (and Grab)

The standing jump is the most basic of Lara's moves. When you do the jump, notice that the two pillars are the exact same height, and that the distance between them is a square sector—a sector in which one of the aforementioned cubes would fit perfectly. If the target pillar were closer, it would have to be taller for Lara to complete a standing jump and grab. If the target were farther away, Lara might still be able to jump and grab it if the target ledge were lower—though she does run out of momentum pretty fast when jumping from the standing position. The ability Lara has to grab ledges and pull up onto them is used in about half the jumps in the game.

3: The Running Jump

Lara should get a running start at a jump in order to travel greater distances, as long as she has a sector's worth of space to start her approach. Walk to the edge of the ledge, tap Lara backward one little hop, and then run forward before quickly pressing and holding the Jump button. Notice that the obstacles Lara jumped between for the second and third parts of the workout are the same distance apart, but Lara needn't grab something that close, as long as she can get a running start.

By running and jumping, Lara can span a certain distance without having to utilize the grab.

One of the things that the obstacle course only touches on is Lara's ability to pull to the top of pillars. We mention it specifically because it comes into play throughout the game, and occasionally you're pulling up from the midst of some perilous terrain: a ledge full of spikes or rolls of barbwire. In that instance, it's essential that you use the Vault button commands: Forward and the Action button. In that way, Lara will jump to the exact height of the ledge above, and start to pull up immediately. If you try to use a combination of jump, grab, and forward to reach a ledge while standing in hazardous terrain, what happens most of the time is that Lara jumps up past the ledge, and attempts to catch it on the way down. Unfortunately, she hits the hazard before her hands can take hold, and some manner of grim impalement occurs.

A NOTE
on Vaulting
or pulling up

4: Running, Jumping, and Grabbing

The meat and potatoes of the *Tomb Raider* experience is the standard Run, Jump, and Grab, as illustrated by obstacle number four. With this move, Lara can span a truly impressive distance. Get used to how that distance looks, and consider that, once again, the height of the target ledge relative to the level from which Lara jumps is also a factor.

The Run, Jump, and Grab is probably Lara's signature move.

A NOTE on Jump Trajectory

An aspect of Lara's jumping ability that isn't touched on in the gym is that the different types of jumps (standing or running) result in differing trajectories. A standing jump has a higher trajectory than a running jump, and a running jump and grab has a still lower arc. The jump with the lowest arc is the backflip. Though it only comes into play occasionally, there are times in the game when a backflip is the only way to defeat a movement puzzle, due purely to the backflip's low arc.

5: The Shimmy

Occasionally, Lara can grab the edge of a surface, but for various reasons, can't pull up to stand atop it. Either the edge is a crack in the wall, in which case there's no room for her to pull up into, or the surface itself is sloped, and she can stand for only an instant before slipping back down to the grab position. In those cases, what's usually called for is a shimmy. Just work your way along the crack in either direction. Eventually, she'll find a safe place to stand on a nearby ledge. During the workout, Lara takes advantage of this opportunity to show how she can step backward off of a ledge, and catch herself before hitting the floor (or dropping to her death, as is often the case). Try this: Stand facing a ledge, but not right at the edge, say about in the center of a sector of space. Roll and grab, and you should hang from the ledge. That's a lot cooler than doing an about-face every time you want to hang from a ledge, though you can't do it from too close to the drop off. Also, notice that when you hang and drop to the ground, you can Roll in order to quickly orient yourself with Lara's back to the wall.

With the shimmy, Lara can hang and move along small cracks in surfaces.

6: Crawling

One of the new moves which Lara displays in *Tomb Raider II* is the ability to crawl in small spaces. She can enter those spaces by hanging and pulling up into them, and also by using the Crouch button, followed by directional arrows to control her movement. Some things to note: When Lara is kneeling, she can't do anything until you use the Forward button to get her into a full crawl, but she can draw her guns or light a Flare while crouched. Also, when Lara is crawling, you can let go of the Crouch button as long as the space confines her to the Crouch. In that way, Lara will stand immediately upon entering an area which would permit her to do so, providing you take your finger off of the Forward Directional button. Of course, some overhead hazard may mean that you don't want her to stand up right away, so consider the circumstances. Which reminds us: Back Lara off the ledge, so that there's nothing above her to keep her crouched. Hit the Crouch button, and then the Look button. It seems like about half the time, for reasons known only to her, Lara will stand up if you try to use the Look command from a crouched position. Just something to keep in mind.

When crawling, back Lara into a hanging position using the Action and Grab buttons.

Climbing and the Monkey Swing

Lara can climb certain textures in *Tomb Raider III*: Though they're not always obvious, they remain relatively consistent within each level. The new trick, performed from the top of the gym climb, is the monkey swing. Just as with a climbable surface, it's not always something so obvious as a ready-made ladder, but the swingable surface textures are pretty consistent within each level. Many, many times in *Tomb Raider II*, you'll reach an apparent dead end. Look up. Chances are there's a monkey swing surface in the vicinity.

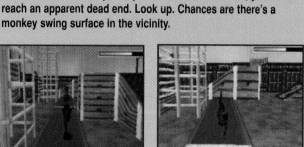

Lara can sprint short distances, which helps her avoid certain traps and defeat certain timed puzzles.

Pressing the Jump button while sprinting can make Lara finish her run with a forward roll: she won't reverse direction as with the standard roll.

Climbing is another means by which Lara overcomes obstacles.

The monkey swing lets Lara travel to places that might seem out of reach.

The Sprint (and Dive)

The last new move for Lara in *Tomb Raider III* is the sprint, which gives our heroine a brief flash of speed. Of course, within the game, that adds a new twist to an old type of puzzle: traps happen faster when there's a timed element, and you must employ the sprint to avoid catastrophe in many instances. Lara can finish her sprint with a nice little rolling dive, though that's only occasionally demanded of her once the game begins. As long as you're sprinting, do a little testing of how that effects Lara's ability to stop and turn. You'll find that turns become much wider, and that stopping while sprinting elicits a small skid. The turning diameter is the factor which most often comes into play within the game.

The Assault Course

Outside of Lara's home is a much larger Assault Course, updated from *Tomb Raider II* to include Lara's new-found abilities. We're not going to go over the course blow for blow, since it's just high-end extrapolation on the techniques learned in the gym. That's the stuff that the game itself teaches you, through trial and error, and the specific in-game situations are addressed in the walkthrough. We did want to point out, however, that the Assault Course is worth a look, even if you're not going to do it for time. The reason: Once you find your pistols in the crawl space, it's time for a little target practice. Not all of the targets are stationary. Go ahead. Check it out.

Lara's Home (Revisited)

As long as you're spending a few minutes knocking around Lara's Home, you might as well solve the couple of puzzles there, just to see what you can see. Try out the Quad Bike on the racetrack, too.

Cool outfit. Been hitting the sherry, have we?

Jeeves starting to irritate you a bit? Come here, old man. Chill out.

The Trophy Room

The first little puzzle is the act of getting into Lara's Trophy Room. On the diving platform near the pool is a button. Press it, and a small alcove near the front door opens. Throw the Switch in the alcove, then roll and sprint, finishing with a dive as the Trophy Room door slides shut. To get out, use the Switch by the door. Twice.

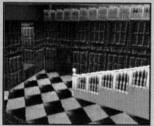

To enter the Trophy Room, first push the button on the diving platform.

Throw the Switch in the alcove to the right of the front door, then sprint and dive for the chamber behind you.

Ah, yes. This brings back memories ....

The Racetrack Key

As you arrive at Lara's home, open up the closet near the bed. It's dark inside, but the space is small: search and find the Flares. On the second floor walkway, above the stairs, is a door with a button beside it. Through the door and up the stairs is the attic. Pop a Flare and discover the movable box. Push it twice.

In the attic, push the box twice.

In the library, look for the protruding book on the right, and push it in.

Go back down to the second floor—leaving the attic door open—and into the library, opposite Lara's bedroom. On the right as you enter, a book protrudes from the book case. Push it in, and the fire in the nearby fireplace goes out.

Climb up through the fireplace.

Push the box to reveal the exit path.

Climb up the chimney, and move the boxes. One is sitting atop more Flares, the other slides to reveal a hallway—that's the box that you pushed earlier in the attic, and the hallway leads back there.

Jump the banisters to save time.

You have to hustle to make it to the basement door before it closes.

Throw the Switch, and a door opens on the first floor, in the short hall leading to the gym. You have to sprint to make it inside, but only sprint in a straight line, or you invariably wind up smacking into a wall. There's no time to spare on smacking. To shave a few seconds off, realize that you can jump the banister straight out of the attic door, run down the stairs a few steps, then jump to the right and roll. A that point, the door that has opened is only a few meters in front of you, on the right.

In the huge aquarium, you can spy the Racetrack Key.

I feel a course record comin' on ....

Down in the basement, move the box over beneath the hole in the ceiling, then jump, grab, and pull up into the hallway. At the end of the hall is an entrance to the gigantic aquarium. In the aquarium is the Racetrack Key. Don't get so caught up swimming with the fish that you run out of air and drown. The entrance to the racetrack is where the hedge maze used to be in *Tomb Raider II*: out the front door and past the statue on the left. Time for a little Quad Bikin'.

Tomb Raider III Combat

Tomb Raider never was about combat. She points, you shoot; everybody gets what they deserve. Still, there are a couple of wrinkles in *Tomb Raider III* that deserve some mention, just so you can't complain about not having been warned. There are also a few basics that we'll cover right off the bat, just so no one gets left behind. Of course, specific in-game situations—nasty ambushes and specific monsters and such—are covered in the game walkthrough.

The Basics

The greatest single advantage Lara has over her enemies is dead simple: The woman has moves. She has skills. She got game. Don't you let her stand there flat footed while some monkey gnaws her kneecaps.

Backflipping

Jumping backward in a straight line is the easiest way to deal with onrushing enemies, especially early in the game. As the adventure progresses, quarters get tighter, enemies get tougher, and you can't always kill them before they catch up to you. Still, the backflip remains a staple for much of the game, especially if there's no danger of taking a nasty fall.

Get a move on, and combat is much easier.

Jumping and Shooting

As you're sure to notice, Lara doesn't need your help to aim at a target. And, once you start firing, that target remains locked as long as you continue to hold down the Fire button. Even if an opponent goes out of view, it is still locked as long as you keep the Fire button held down. What that means, in practical terms, is that Lara can jump around like mad, and, as long as you keep that Fire button held, she'll squeeze off shots whenever the target happens to be in front of her. Don't try to put so much thought into your jumping display that you never get a shot off. Jump crazily, randomly, rolling and running and spinning in mid-air. As long as there is no hazardous terrain in the area, and that Fire button is down, things will work out.

Elevation Conserves Ammo

Throughout the game, you'll come into some area and be bush-whacked—surprised by some sudden threat and in imminent danger. Consider that sometimes discretion is indeed the better part of valor. At the very least, a little discretion can save a ton of ammo. If you seek higher ground, as opposed to slugging it out on even footing, you can assault the enemy from above using just your Pistols. Sure, you may have to hop down to a foe's level to draw it out into the open, but get right back up on your high perch, and plink away. That'll help you conserve the best types of ammo for those enemies who are truly deserving: those which don't have to rely purely on ambushing you in order to present a serious threat to Lara's health.

Roll and shoot to get those nasty birds out of your hair.

Feeling a Little Sick?

Another new aspect of the *Tomb Raider II* experience is the ability that some foes have to poison Lara. The damage that these attacks do is not a threat in and of itself, but the long-term prognosis is not good. Lara's health meter begins to flash yellow, and slowly her life drains away. A Medi Pack of any size will correct the poisoning, but consider: When you first get poisoned, there may be other enemies in the immediate area that have that same capability. It behooves you to make a quick run through the surroundings—be it beside a river, in the desert, or near the gorge ... whatever—and try to draw out any more foes with poisoning on their mind. Few things push the ol' suckometer further into the red than using a Medi Pack really quickly, then stepping around the next turn in the hall and getting poisoned again right away.

Don't Forget the Roll

One of the most overlooked of Lara's moves, the roll has a variety of uses, none more important than when it's used as part of combat. If you're rolling back and forth—or rolling and backflipping over and over again—most enemies without a distance attack have a hard time getting close to you. Also, when your back is to the wall, the panicked tendency is to jump lamely straight up and down. Not a good thing. Roll and backflip.

Monster Notes

Ah, if we only knew then what we know now. Despite the relatively straightforward approach which Lara brings to combat situations, and the similarly aggressive nature of the enemies you encounter, there are a couple of things that stand out. Most of the specific monster information is included with the walkthrough of the level where each type appears, but we wanted to get a couple of things up front.

Snakes in the Grass

One of the new monster-specific traps you'll find in *Tomb Raider II* is snakes hiding in thick grass, or coiled around bushes. In any area where you can't be sure what might be lying in wait, the best course of action is to walk slowly. The snake will rise up as you approach, but it won't strike immediately. From that point, you can hop backward and open fire.

There are snakes waiting for an unwary adventurer. Proceed with caution.

A New Breed of Crocodile

If at all possible, pop that croc from the shore.

The king-size crocs of *Tomb Raider III* bear little resemblance to earlier versions in that these are extremely aggressive and inflict huge amounts of damage. Occasionally, you have to get into the water with one of these beasts, specifically in the Mudubu Gorge level. Don't linger. Get ashore in a hurry, and don't go in the water without out a firm plan on how you intend to make the safety of the land nearby.

The Shivas

Late in the India hub, you encounter huge statues which bear a striking resemblance to the multi-limbed god, Shiva. These creatures are the worst, as they not only have a serious multi-limbed attack, but they can also cross their swords in front of them to deflect Lara's bullets. The best trick we found for defeating these guys is quite a good one, however. Basically, run right at them. Nutty, we know, but try it out. If you run right at the Shiva firing your Pistols—and you should be using Pistols—the beast takes a few hits, then it crosses it's swords and stands there. With its swords crossed, the beast is immobile. But, when you get right up close to it (not underneath it, mind you, but up close) it'll uncross its arms to swipe at you. As soon as the monster breaks its defensive posture, hop backward and start shooting again. Just one hop usually takes you out of harm's way, as the beast quickly re-crosses its swords to fend off the bullets. And stands there. Rinse and repeat.

Snipers

Many of Lara's foes are armed and quite dangerous, but those sporting a laser sight on their rifle are the worst. Not only do they do big damage when Lara gets shot, but they almost invariably squeeze off a final shot from their knees. That last bullet whacks away about a quarter of the health meter. Seek cover, either by crouching behind something or jumping off to one side, and lean

on the Desert Eagle as the means to a quick kill. You can also use the MP5, and then rattle off another 10 or so bullets after the bad guy drops to his knees. That'll keep him from getting off that last shot in most instances.

Does everyone have days this bad?

Terror From the Skies

More so than in previous *Tomb Raider* games, flying enemies have a real tendency to get above Lara, and drop straight down. This makes it very hard to get a bead on them. As long as you're not on some precarious ledge, use the roll action to open up a small gap, and quickly find the target. You may have to roll and fire several times, but that's the fastest way to get those things out of a girl's hair.

GAMEPLAY BASICS

Lara's Arsenal

Again, this isn't rocket science stuff: big, mean enemies call for heavy artillery. If you conserve by using the Pistols whenever possible, running out of ammo should be a very small concern. Still, there are some nuances to employing the arsenal that bear mention.

MP5

A very cool machine gun, which takes the place of *Tomb Raider II*'s M-16. Like the M-16, however, you have to be standing flat-footed when you fire. Any acrobatics or even a simple backstep, and the gun goes inactive. That can be very bad. Try to use the MP5 to pick off distant targets, specifically against targets with ranged attacks of their own. Lean on the MP5 when fighting raptors and snipers.

Desert Eagle

The Desert Eagle is a single pistol that delivers a very powerful round: two slugs is enough to kill just about anything. Try not to use the Eagle, with the possible exception of nearby raptors, until it's late in the game. You'll appreciate the firepower that much more as the enemies get tougher.

Uzis

Like Pistols, except about five times faster. Very effective. Again, be conservative early in the game, and you can mow through Antarctica like nobody's business.

Grenade Launcher

The Grenade Launcher in *Tomb Raider III* is a mixed bag. Unlike the launcher in *Tomb Raider II*, this variety arms at very short distances. Unfortunately, it's very hard to hit anything more than about 15 meters away. Use it to fire into hallways and small rooms or areas that will contain the grenade. Otherwise, the shell will likely bounce far away from the intended target.

Rocket Launcher

As you might suspect, this is the big enchilada. Don't use it without very good cause: there's only a handful of rockets in the entire game.

Saving the Game

Knowing where to save the game is a big part of completing each level.

The *Tomb Raider III* scheme for saving the game is a hybrid of the schemes employed in the first two games. Now, you collect Save Crystals in limited numbers, and then are tasked with using them expediently throughout a level. Of course, until you actually experience each level—or read our notes in the walkthrough section—it's hard to know where those good save places are. A bit of it is relative in that different people get freaked out by different types of obstacles or jumps. This certainly comes into play when deciding where to save. The one generalization we're willing to make is to save very infrequently in the early stages of the game—we save once at the halfway point of the first level, just as a precaution. This way you can pad your crystal total, which really helps as the puzzles get harder, and the levels get bigger, later in the game.

About This Book

The walkthrough structure of this book is very picture-intensive, and hopefully that's all you'll need to make it through each level. It's kind of a visual nudge in the right direction. For more specific insights, check the boxed text on each page. The boxes pertain directly to the nearby screenshots, provide a level of detail that doesn't fit well in a caption.

The order of the three central hubs presented here isn't random, but it's certainly not the only way to get through the game. We took Nevada second since we figured it was better to bite the bullet sooner than later: all of your stuff gets taken away at the start of the second level, and, unlike *Tomb Raider I*, you don't find some skateboarder a few minutes later who happens to be holding 10 Uzi clips.

So it's Nevada first, and then the South Pacific Islands. That was really a toss up. Could have been London. London is dark and rainy. The South Pacific just seemed so appealing. Those levels are tough, though, especially Mudubu Gorge. Flip a coin, but realize that if you go in a different order than in the book, you'll notice a slight variation in where you come across certain weapons. Make sure you hit all the Secret areas, and everything works out fine. This is another major point of interest: you need to find every last Secret in the game in order to access the Secret Level—All Hallows—at the end of the game. Don't settle for anything less.

GAMEPLAY BASICS

India
Jungle
Temple Ruins
The River Ganges
Caves of Kaliya

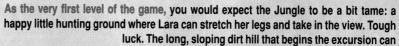

SECRET
6 secrets

As the very first level of the game, you would expect the Jungle to be a bit tame: a happy little hunting ground where Lara can stretch her legs and take in the view. Tough luck. The long, sloping dirt hill that begins the excursion can be a painful experience, and there are plenty more where that came from once you finally make it to solid ground. From a combat standpoint, a few tigers are the most you have to worry about, and there's usually a way to get a height advantage in those battles. Try to use Medi Packs, as opposed to Save Crystals, and you can hoard those crystals for later in the game when the Jungle is but a fond memory of how simple and easy things used to be. If you fall in the river at any point, don't try to fight the current. Go with the flow, and avoid the pockets of piranha. At the far end of the river is a small underwater tunnel that allows you to backtrack after a misstep.

1

SECRET

Getting down the big dirt slope isn't so bad (once you've done it a couple of times). Sliding down forward is a big key, and it's nice to have that little flat spot to stop and take stock of things. By the time you reach the bottom, you should have the level's first two secrets. If not, try again. Get used to the undulating motion caused by the quicksand: that's the graphical tip-off, as not all of the quicksand looks the same. Also, go ahead and light a Flare, or three. In the first two levels of the game, there are a ton of Flares, especially if you're picking the packs from the hollow trees, and hitting all the Secrets.

2

Don't slide down the large dirt hill until you nab the level's first secret. Jump up and over the slope on your right as the level gets underway, and slide down onto the green ledge.

Stand at the edge of the green ledge and jump toward the right-hand tip of the yellowish rock. Ducking down below the canopy, you can spy the **Shotgun**, and also look down the dirt slope.

Sliding down the dirt slope, jump up and grab the overhead log. Dispose of the monkey, and line up as you see here before hanging and dropping from the back of the log to the slope once more.

Let Lara slide to a stop. If you lined up properly, you should stop in a small spike-free section. Jump toward the wall on the left to continue downward.

Sliding down near the wall, you can reach the ledge below and not have to worry about the boulder that releases when you go for the Large Medi Pack.

From the ledge with the boulder, walk to the right of the tree. Jump from there past the tree, leaning to the left in midair.

SECRET

SECRET

Past the tree, a Save Crystal and some ammo wait on a high ledge. Return back the way you came, jumping around the tree to the ledge near the boulder.

From the ledge with the boulder, run back onto the slope facing forward. Jump across the last row of spikes, hugging the wall on Lara's left.

Collect the Save Crystal, but walk carefully in this area, as most of it is a quicksand mire. Jump, grab, and pull up to the top of the pillar just past the crystal.

In the area above the Save Crystal, collect the prizes from the watery nooks.

The first relatively complicated puzzle of the game involves a wall of spikes in a small, dark room. Throw the switch on the wall, roll, and then run across to the safety of the window sill. Use the Action button to climb quickly out of harm's way. Roll again as soon as she makes the sill, holding down the Roll button once Lara starts to climb so that she doesn't hesitate too long. Back off the sill carefully, as the spike trap is double sided.

3

From the solid ground near where you found the Save Crystal, you can wade to a short hall. In the open area, shoot the monkey before he runs off with the Small Medi Pack on the patio.

Check the river through a narrow passage on the right where you spied the larcenous monkey. The current is strong, and the water is filled with piranha.

Down a hallway off the monkey's patio is a switch to throw. Do notice the view of the river from there.

Throwing the switch at the end of the short hallway opens the door on the ledge above the patio.

When you throw the switch in the dark chamber, a wall of spikes closes in from Lara's left.

4

Across the level's first rope slide, a tiger attacks in the darkened jungle area; it can be nasty. If you enter the area and move quickly to face the log on the left, you can jump atop it, though you have to jump up and over the log's steep, sloping side to reach an area where Lara can stand. Realistically, you have time for one good attempt, and then you're better off just leaping around the area—to the right as you came in—and plinking away at the tiger. If you have to use a Small Medi Pack, so be it. In order to access the long pathway off the jungle area, you must first throw the switch inside the tree, which releases a boulder from the hill above. Climb the steps on the left once you throw the switch, and all's well. A second switch up the hill opens the long pathway.

Throw the switch, roll, and run for the safety of the sill behind you. Climb quickly and roll. When the wall passes, use the rope slide on the newly accessible ledge.

Through the hole in the huge tree, expect tiger trouble as you enter the open area.

If you move fast, you can jump up over the sloped side of the log on the left, and fight from atop it. Otherwise, you have to get mobile, and fight the kitty from ground level.

In the same area where the tiger attacks, you can jump up a greenish slope and collect ammo.

Defend against the resident monkeys, and throw the switch inside the tree, mindful of the impending boulder. Investigate the area where the boulder first sat to find a second switch near a gate.

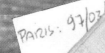

On the long pathway, notice that the first cat doesn't like to venture out of the main pathway. Backflip straight back down the path as he advances, and it's only the second kitty that's cause for concern. It appears when you approach the far end of the pathway, emerging from between the two pillars. Keep backflipping and firing. You may get damaged, but less so if you're anticipating the attack and moving backward as the big cat appears. Do note that you can pass through the hedge on the right, where the slope is dirty, and gather ammo. If you're not really comfortable leaping back and forth above a spiked pit, you might save the game before entering the secret log. It's not too tough to escape the trap, but it's unnerving and can be quite deadly if you make a mistake.

5

6

Once you backtrack around to the ledge near the secret log's entrance, the next order of business is to climb the tall cliff down the nearby passage and across a spiked section of floor. The climb itself is straightforward, with a small sidetrip to snag that tantalizing Save Crystal. The cave at the top of the cliff, past a small shimmy, is a typical boulder-in-a-hallway trap, but it's the cave's darkness that makes the trap deadly. After you throw the switch in the hall and begin to make your way back to the entrance, the boulder falls behind you. We strongly recommend throwing a flare (or two) near the entrance to the cave once you kill the monkey. That way, when you're running back, the entrance—now the emergency exit—glows. There is no need to sprint to beat the boulder, and arresting your momentum from the sprint mode can be hard to do when you need to make that sharp right-hand turn.

Backflipping or bouncing off the sloped sides of the area, can help you dodge the kitties. The second tiger appears when you approach the far end of the path. Notice there is an area where you can pass through the hedge.

Past the path of the tigers, a monkey waits in a fog-shrouded clearing. Avoid the spiked pit, and don't overlook the ammo near the trees on the right.

Crawl beneath the fallen tree and follow the path to climb atop it. Expect more tiger trouble near the Save Crystal.

SECRET

From the edge of the ledge, facing the log, you can jump forward and grab the edge of the entrance to a secret chamber inside the log. Getting out is a tricky.

Hanging and dropping from the secret log, you'll fall into a nasty trap below. Keep jumping back and forth to avoid the spikes, and keep leaning to one side to eventually jump clear of the slopes.

After you collect the ammo (two servings) from the rocks near the entrance, drop down into the tunnel and walk to the far wall amidst the spikes. Pull up to the ledge above to escape: *do not* jump and grab, use the action and forward buttons.

Backtrack around to the area near the secret log entrance, and follow the lattice-work hallway to a spiked ledge. Shoot the monkey prowling the cliff face, and walk through the spikes.

Run, jump, and grab to reach a distant outside corner of the latticed hall. From there, jump to the slope above the hallway, slide backward and grab the edge. Shimmy all the way to the right (above the spikes) before pulling up to claim the Save Crystal.

Climb and shimmy to the high, dark cave. If you throw a flare near the entrance, it's easier to spot the exit when the boulder is chasing you. Hurt the monkey and throw the switch. The boulder falls from above when you double back down the hallway.

SECRET

If you jump up near the switch in the boulder hallway, you can grab a ledge above. Pull up and claim the ammo, then crawl backward and use the Action button to lower Lara back to the hallway. The gate that the switch opens is at ground level of the outside area. Expect tiger trouble.

7 The jungle area where the boulders roll down from the bushes isn't particularly tough (big tip: *Get out of the way!*) but the Secret is brutal, especially the first time you see it—unless you follow along carefully. Getting down to the Secret is simple enough: you back into the hole near that Small Medi Pack, and hang. Let go of the Action button and quickly press it again as Lara falls. She should catch the edge of the ledge below, just above a spiked floor. Collect the goodies from the hallway, and return to the edge of the ledge which you grabbed from above. Notice the slope of the ceiling. Stand to the far right side of the ledge. Jump forward and grab (you won't grab anything, but you need to do the motion to adjust Lara's trajectory downward a bit). From the surface where you land, pivot and move to the edge of the ledge facing the entrance to the secret hall. Jump forward and grab, and you should catch the ledge up above. Pull up to safety.

In the jungle area, a monkey leads you toward a boulder trap. Two boulders roll out initially, and then a third starts when you investigate up the hill toward the bushes. Climb the extreme right side of the hill, jumping a slope to reach the bushes.

Behind the bushes, you find a small area with a hole in the floor. Back into the hole (near a Small Medi Pack) and grab the pointy ledge. Drop and grab as you fall to catch the ledge below. Pull up. See box 7 about getting back out.

Explore the river area. There is ammo, and no piranha. There's also a shortcut near the island, under the water.

You have to leap to the small central island, then jump up from the square sector to grab the ledge above.

Throwing the switch on the upper ledge opens the door high on the wall in the background.

To reach the door, run, jump, and grab from the small island to a flat spot just to the right of the pillar.

Ride the rope slider across the chasm to the hallway and follow the passage to the left.

From atop a pillar you can reach the Save Crystal unmolested, but expect double tiger trouble when you venture into the large outer area. You can coax the tigers out of hiding by jumping atop the pillar, as shown here.

In order to reach the opening on the right side of the falls, you must flood the huge area. Investigate the dark passage to the left of the falls.

Cross the pool, and turn to the right on the ledge near the distant sealed portal. Don't overlook the Flares on the central platform.

8 Just in case you're playing the level for time, we mention the shortcut off of the large watery area where you climb the small island and throw the switch on the upper ledge. If you swim through, you go directly to a room with two switches on either end of a walkway. Of course, you miss out on a second rope slider for no good reason in the process. We figured you'd want the long version. The jump from the island to the rocks near the wall is tricky. Run, jump, and grab the flat rock just to the right of the right-hand pillar. Below that point is the shortcut, just in case you lose faith.

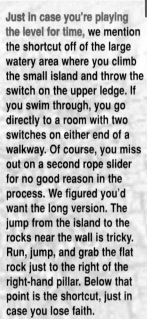

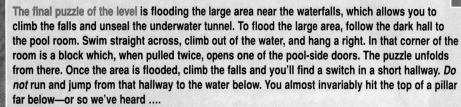

The final puzzle of the level is flooding the large area near the waterfalls, which allows you to climb the falls and unseal the underwater tunnel. To flood the large area, follow the dark hall to the pool room. Swim straight across, climb out of the water, and hang a right. In that corner of the room is a block which, when pulled twice, opens one of the pool-side doors. The puzzle unfolds from there. Once the area is flooded, climb the falls and you'll find a switch in a short hallway. *Do not* run and jump from that hallway to the water below. You almost invariably hit the top of a pillar far below—or so we've heard ....

To the right of the aforementioned sealed portal is a block you must pull twice. The portal should open. Inside is a switch that opens a trapdoor behind the block.

Swim down behind the block and surface at a walkway. Throw the switches at either end of the walkway.

Return to the outer pool and throw the switch behind the second unsealed portal. The large area near the waterfalls floods. Now you can return and swim to the ledge that had been out of reach.

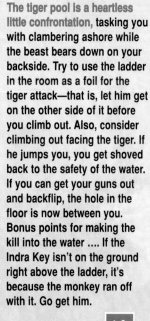

The tiger pool is a heartless little confrontation, tasking you with clambering ashore while the beast bears down on your backside. Try to use the ladder in the room as a foil for the tiger attack—that is, let him get on the other side of it before you climb out. Also, consider climbing out facing the tiger. If he jumps you, you get shoved back to the safety of the water. If you can get your guns out and backflip, the hole in the floor is now between you. Bonus points for making the kill into the water .... If the Indra Key isn't on the ground right above the ladder, it's because the monkey ran off with it. Go get him.

Follow the path up the falls. You find a hallway with a switch to throw. Be careful not to hit any solid ground if you leap from high up near the falls.

Follow the underwater passage now open off of the flooded area.

When you surface, you'll be floating in a pool with a tiger lurking nearby. Wait for him to back off a bit before climbing ashore, and get mobile in the small area. Keep jumping side-to-side, rolling, and firing: there is no good place to hide.

When the tiger finally bleeds out, check the immediate area for ammo, and climb the ladder.

Up the ladder, a monkey tries to make off with the Indra Key. Bad monkey. Die.

From the upper ledge, dispose of the tiger. From this angle, the tiger is less likely to seek cover.

Collect the ammo from the small alcove to the left of the door, then apply the Indra Key to the lock. Slog through the quicksand to make your exit.

India

SECRET

4 secrets

The Temple Ruins are sprawling with deadly mudslides, so you have some work to do just getting into the temple proper. The large cobras hiding in the bushes when the level begins are poisonous, so coax them up into a striking stance, and then step quickly backward to kill them from a safe distance. There are two in that initial area, one on the far side of the hole through the tree, and one farther along the rock wall in the direction of the trapdoor shortcut switch. In the small system of tunnels, another cobra lurks around a corner to the left: stick to the right-hand wall, and look before you proceed around the corner. Walk carefully forward to roust the snake and step quickly back. When you cross the river with the central platform, you'll have to run, jump, and grab to make it to the relative safety of the partially submerged walkway. If you don't grab in midair, the piranhas have more of a tendency to nip our heroine's heals. Finally, when you jump into the water to swim through the passage opened by the switch, back off and leap in so that you sink more quickly and hopefully avoid the fiendish fish. Ready, set, go!

1

Having rid the area of cobras, check the river. There's an underwater opening, but piranhas are on the prowl. In the corner of the small area is a switch which lets you bypass the water.

Follow the underground passage, wary of a cobra around a blind corner, and emerge near another section of river. Claim the ammo and notice the central platform.

Run, jump, and grab starting from the roots of the tree so you can catch the edge of the platform. From there, you can run and jump to the distant walkway.

2

Go through the underwater tunnel, which opened when you threw the previous switch. You emerge in a large outdoor area where two monkeys prowl. Climb the block at the far end of the large area and grab the ledge above. Find some ammo. Continue along the upper walkway, and notice the ammo on the ledge to the left of the doorway. If you press face-first against the wall, hop back once, and then take two steps forward, you can reach it. From that position, turn to the left slightly so that you can run and jump without hitting the wall. Hop backward once to set up the run distance and lean to the right and grab in midair. You should land near the ammo. In the treetops, take the elevation of the surfaces into account when you jump. To get to the Flares, jump from the small triangular section and around the tree trunk on the right. Run, jump, then lean to the left as you leap and you'll catch the root ramp on the far side of the tree. Hang a right at the root ramp, jump to the slope, and you're there. There's also ammo to the left as you come beneath the tree canopy. It's considerably easier to obtain.

Throwing the switch at the end of the walkway opens an underwater passage. Back off from the break in the walkway and jump into the water so that you sink quickly.

Follow the underwater passage. You surface in a large area near a mudslide. Kill the monkeys and climb to the upper ledge, where you might leap for a tricky stash of ammo.

This is a good place to save the game. The trees on the left are full of goodies, but the odds are you'll slip and fall when looking around. The backtracking gets tedious.

In the trees you'll even find (*yes!*) some more Flares, if you look hard enough.

Once you've pilfered the treetops, continue toward the waterfall, running, jumping, and grabbing onto the white platform and then to the Small Medi Pack near the tree. Follow the passage and slide backward to shimmy across the falls.

After disposing of the monkey, crawl into the crack on the extreme left-hand side. There's a snake waiting in the darkness just through the opening.

Follow the tunnels, wary of another cobra at a blind turn to the right. Slide down the run near the right-hand wall to avoid the boulder, and you'll enter the temple.

The animated Shiva statues make for fearsome foes, as they display a new tactic in *Tomb Raider* terms: a defensive posture. Their small weakness is that they can only cross their blades in front of them and stay immobile with the blades crossed. Sometimes that allows you to get behind them and do good damage before they turn. Still, a much safer tactic would have to be the semi-tedious task of bating them into dropping their guard, and then climbing back up to a safe location to squeeze off a couple of shots. In the case of the first monster, you can hop from the ledge and climb back up, or run around in the large area just for the cinematic appeal. Use the sprint mode to open up a good gap if the monster gets too close. Notice that the level's path diverges at the first Shiva room. You have to take both routes to get both Ganesha Keys, but the order is arbitrary. The path we chose first is more demanding, perhaps, but finding the switch that floods the small pool—the other route—poses an even greater challenge.

3

4

When you come into the chamber with the Save Crystal on the ledge, the distant Shiva animates. Climb the ledge to safety.

From the ledge where the crystal sat, plink away at the monster. If you hop down off the ledge and back up again, he'll drop his guard. Throw the two switches at either end of the ledge.

The two switches open a door at ground level. The other door is opened by a switch in the small area in front of it.

When you throw the single switch which opens the door above, turn to the right and push the wall to enter a secret area. Crawl beneath the dart traps and don't go in the hole.

Through the door opened by the single switch, the tunnel turns to mud. Unless you run and jump from the edge of the solid floor and begin slogging immediately down the hallway, you sink down and take a bit of damage before re-surfacing.

Doubling back above the mud-filled hall—run and jump to grab the ledge—you'll find a monkey to kill and a switch to throw. This is a good place to save the game (See box 4).

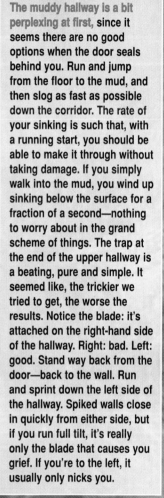

The muddy hallway is a bit perplexing at first, since it seems there are no good options when the door seals behind you. Run and jump from the floor to the mud, and then slog as fast as possible down the corridor. The rate of your sinking is such that, with a running start, you should be able to make it through without taking damage. If you simply walk into the mud, you wind up sinking below the surface for a fraction of a second—nothing to worry about in the grand scheme of things. The trap at the end of the upper hallway is a beating, pure and simple. It seemed like, the trickier we tried to get, the worse the results. Notice the blade: it's attached on the right-hand side of the hallway. Right: bad. Left: good. Stand way back from the door—back to the wall. Run and sprint down the left side of the hallway. Spiked walls close in quickly from either side, but if you run full tilt, it's really only the blade that causes you grief. If you're to the left, it usually only nicks you.

SECRET

In the room with the two monkeys, you can push the block to reach a high ledge—not the one with the obvious door. From there, you can jump and grab a ladder up through a hole in the ceiling. Take the goodies and throw the switch.

Lower Lara back down the ladder as far as she'll go, and drop to the floor from the secret area. She'll take a small bit of damage.

By pushing the same block which allowed you to reach the secret area, you can easily reach the door which opens using the switch below. Drop into the pool and throw the switch. Get a good breath before going through the underwater door.

Swim down the underwater passage and turn right as it widens. Swim to the switch on the wall, then pull it and roll. Swim straight to the other end of the chamber and you'll find another switch to pull.

5 Past the diabolical hallway trap, you enter a room with two monkeys prowling at floor level. To the right, as you enter, is a large block you can push around in a limited area. On the far side of the central construct is a switch that opens a door on one upper ledge. By using the block to stand on, you can reach that ledge, and also another higher perch. On the uppermost walkway, you should spy a dark tunnel leading up into the ceiling. Jump to the ladder from the edge of the walkway and climb up to the secret chamber. You have to throw the switch up there in order to access the next secret area, which is farther into the level—you'll get a brief glimpse. The key to getting past the water puzzles—opening the trapdoor in the ceiling of the underwater passage and collecting the goodies from the aforementioned secret area—is getting a full breath at the last possible minute. For the first puzzle, get a breath and then swim down through the door. Try to stick to the center of the irregular passage. Also, realize that when you throw the first switch, you need make no adjustments to your course. Just roll and swim straight forward and you'll arrive neatly at switch number two.

Once you've pulled both underwater switches in the large area, double back down the passage you came from and look for an opening in the ceiling about halfway down.

SECRET

In the huge chamber where you surface, there is a lone switch on one wall of the pool. Get a good breath, pull it, and roll. Swim across the pool to the timed door slightly to the right. Once inside, there are three pick-ups to claim, then the door opens to allow you to leave.

The other switches in the pool cause the statues to billow fire, revealing translucent platforms. Turn off the statues, and use a Flare as your guide. Jump and grab the platform from the side where you find the Save Crystal.

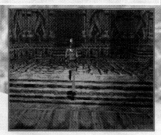

From the translucent platform, jump to the ledge and throw the switch. Quickly jump left, then turn and step off the edge of the ledge, leaning to the right to catch the ground below. Sprint through the timed door.

This is a good place to save. When you throw the switch, turn immediately to the left, and sprint down the wide hallway.

6 Getting the Ganesha Key from the wide, dark hallway is a sprint puzzle with some very demanding parameters, especially regarding the time it takes you to stop running while in the sprint mode. Even knowing where the key is, it's tough to arrest your momentum in the vicinity of the prize. Consider that it's much better to ease up on the throttle—so to speak—early, as opposed to late. You still need to sprint 90 percent of the distance, but if you drop back to standard run as you approach the key, it's easier to stop right on top of it. That can save a heck of a lot of time. Getting out before the wall seals off the escape route also requires the sprint. A relatively wide loop can let you line up better with the door. Regarding the boulder trap in the hallway: the boulder releases when you touch the second stair, rounding a corner to the right. Get the Flares from the nook (where the boulder will stop), then stand on the first step and roll to trigger the trap. Light the left-hand turn with one of those handy Flares to aid your escape.

A Ganesha Key—one of two—sits at the far end of the hallway, to the left. Grab it and roll, then sprint back down the hallway toward the spiked wall. The door through which you entered is open, if you can make it before the wall passes that point.

Wade through the mud, sticking to the sides of the chamber to avoid falling debris.

Follow the mudslide up the hill, leaping over two sets of slopes to a hallway with a nasty boulder trap (See box 6). Past the boulder the hallway divides. Choose the right-hand path.

Continue in the hallway, putting a significant dent in the local monkey population and claiming another Save Crystal. Climb down the ladder and drop from the bottom back into the room with the Ganesha Keys door.

Go through the door the two switches opened on the ledge and dispose of the monkeys near the dry pool. The second Ganesha Key is down a hallway off the pool. To open the hallway, you have to flood the pool. Save the game.

INDIA

Another Ganesha Key waits down a pathway off of a dry pool. You need to flood the pool in order to throw the "underwater" switch located in the pool. Though this route has several minor traps, it's not nearly as complex as the previous venture. The big trick is finding the switch to flood the pool. And we already know where it is. Getting the underwater passageway open is a little harrowing, but workable. Hug the lower right-hand side of the tunnel on the way there and use that same side (except it'll be the left) on the way back. Otherwise, on the way back, you tend to run into the open door, and get deflected into the path of the dart trap. Hug the right-hand wall in the chamber to avoid falling debris and climb the walls. When you get to the ledge with the snake, you might consider saving. It almost invariably poisons you, so that's not too big a concern, but there's also a boulder that threatens to squash you when you make the final standing jump to the doorway (run inside and make a quick right).

Swim across the pool with the flaming statues. Pull up at the far end while the flames are in full-force. They'll wane as you emerge. Throw the switch and backflip to the pool as things heat up again.

Stick to the lower right-hand corner of the underwater passage and hug the right-hand wall very tightly in the chamber beyond. Climb out onto the ledge with the Small Medi Pack as the ceiling falls in.

Cross the pool and climb the ladders and ledges. You'll have to backflip from the top of the first ladder, and jump to catch the second one.

Ah yes, the pool switch. Past the blades, pick up the Save Crystal and push the block to the right into the wall. Turn to the right and push that block all the way down and out into an open area. That area is one big, nasty boulder trap. About face. Notice the off-colored block at the end of the long hallway—the hallway you created by pushing the second block into the outer area. Push that off-colored block in. To the immediate left of that first block is another, but don't move that one yet. Pass by that block to the next in line, and push that one in, as well. Now you can push the central block aside—into the space where the off-colored block first sat. Throw the switch. Double back in the direction you came from to find the secret area. Pay particular attention that you drop into the pit as shown.

Take elevation into account as you climb. The jumps which require running first are all obviously long distances. The ones that look questionable are the stand-and-jump variety. (See box 7 about the snake ledge.)

In the chamber where you dodge to avoid the boulder upon arrival, crawl beneath the darts and blades to the edge of the pit. Jump and grab the distant ledge.

When you pick up the Save Crystal, turn to the right. There's a movable block in the wall. Push it in, then turn to the right again and push the block there. Push it all the way into an open area, if you like, but don't explore in that tunnel. It's a deathtrap.

By pushing the block out into the large tunnel, you create a hallway. Manipulating the movable blocks that form one side of the hallway, you can reveal the switch that floods the pool near the second Ganesha Key.

Once you throw the switch that fills the pool, return to the room with the two swinging blades. Jump back across the chasm. Stand in this corner to hang and drop to the area below.

From the corner where you drop into the pit, crawl through the razor grass to a small opening.

SECRET

Follow the tunnel from the razor grass pit, hugging the left-hand wall when you must crawl again. Take out the cobra, and collect the prizes. Jump from the opening to the water far below, and backtrack to the flooded pool.

The final leg of the level before the last two traps is pretty straight-forward, though it can be a little stressful. As long as you jump the gap beyond the Ganesha Keys door, you should be able to climb faster than the ceiling falls. Roll at the top to quickly get clear of the spikes, and be mindful that even a monkey can kill you if your health is low. As you enter that room, the block you can pull is to the right in the corner. Run, jump, and grab the upper ledge, then throw the two switches. When you drop back down, sprint across the room to coax two boulders from the opened door. When you sprint past the flaming statues, do so at an angle toward the corner, otherwise you'll likely stumble to stop in the danger zone while trying to make the turn.

9

After retrieving the second Ganesha Key, you can apply them to the locks on either side of the huge portal. The trap beyond is deadly, though it's surmountable … To save or not to save?

Run and jump across the pit beyond the Ganesha Keys door and immediately begin to climb the ladder as the spiked ceiling falls. As long as you don't slip up, you should have just enough time to make the ledge above. Roll and watch out for the monkeys, especially if you get nicked.

In the room with the monkeys and the Save Crystal, you'll have to pull out a block. Then run and jump from atop it to reach a ledge with two switches. In the hallway which opens, use the sprint to get past the flaming statues.

Use the high ledge to help plink away at the pair of Shivas. If you back off the ledge and grab it, then pull back up, the monsters will drop their guard.

When the Shivas finally succumb, take a Scimitar from each and place them in the empty hands of the statue on the ledge. The door below opens.

In the large area, don't climb the central steps just yet. As long as you stay clear of the steps, the boss Shiva won't activate.

Round the corner and take the Save Crystal. The two puzzles before the boss battle are nasty little traps, so save the game (See box 10).

The underwater puzzles tasks you with avoiding a current that wants to suck you into walls of spikes. Fight the current to get over near the wall, and then let it carry you along (See box 10).

The spiked ceiling in the small room is merciless. By sprinting into the room and throwing the switch on the far wall first, you should have just enough time to throw the second switch and step into the hole in the floor that opens (See box 10).

Battling the boss Shiva is a grim task, but it would be more so if the boss didn't avoid the central steps. Use the sprint to open up a gap, keeping the steps between you until you can line up an attack run. Remember the exposed back.

The last two puzzles in the level are killers, plain and simple. When it comes to saving the game, consider saving it near the small dark gate, which opens when you approach. That's a timed puzzle, and it'll probably take a few tries. Save the game there, but run over and figure out the water current puzzle first. You can get that one pretty easily. If you save over there, however, then you have to run all the way back to the dark door when that trap kills you (again and again). The water puzzle is simple in theory. The current attempts to carry you toward walls of spikes. By fighting the current, and edging toward the wall, you can get pulled to a safe area next to the spikes, and thus throw a switch. From there, roll and swim along the wall, low to the floor. The current will start to suck at you again, but you should be able to fight through it and reach the switch near the opposite spiked wall. Once both switches have been thrown, you can claim the first of three Ganesha Keys from the area below the entrance. The dark room requires you to throw two switches before a ceiling of spikes does its dirty work. Back way off from the door—mindful not to step up on the central platform in the large room, and sprint for the opening. You want to be going at full speed when you trigger the ceiling, so you need a long running start. Throw the switch on the wall, roll, and loop to the left to find the second switch. Whether you live or die depends on hitting the switch cleanly, as you have no time to spare. Turn to the right and run into the trapdoor, and the second key is yours. To get the third key, you only need defeat the merciless Shiva boss. Use the sprint when he gets close, and realize that he avoids going up on the steps. Use that impediment to set up your attack runs.

10

PARIS: 97/03

I N D I A

India

Jungle

Temple Ruins

The River Ganges

Caves of Kaliya

SECRET 5 secrets

The River Ganges has two intriguing little twists, the first of which—the Quad Bike— is evident from the get-go. The other twist is that the level has two distinct paths—a shortcut and a main route. We cover both of them here. Consider that, since the main route is the only way to get all the Secrets, that's probably the one you'll choose. In that light, we cover the shortcut first, pointing out where it diverges from the main route and where it joins back up again. If you're going to skip the shortcut entirely, you'll have to skip those pages in the walkthrough, and pick it up at the critical juncture. Finally, take note: There is no good reason to even think about going in the river. You will die. That is all.

1

2

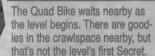

The Quad Bike waits nearby as the level begins. There are goodies in the crawlspace nearby, but that's not the level's first Secret.

Check the ramp that leads— sort of—toward the far opening. Don't take the trip without the first Secret.

From near the ramp, back off the ledge and grab. You should find a group of ladders which takes you to the left.

The first Secret in the level is a bit brutal, since you have to notice it before you go over the very first jump or you're out of luck. The series of jumps tests just about everything you know about Lara's trajectory. Watch your head, and watch that jump after the backflip. It looks short enough to make without running, but you're going to bonk your head about halfway across the river. Run and jump or the deflection sends you into the drink. And don't forget that one on the way back. When it comes to the Quad Bike, proceed with caution in unfamiliar territory. Most importantly, realize that you can hold the brake, and then gun the engine to get your RPMs way up before trying a jump. Also, if you put the back of the Quad Bike to the wall in preparation for a jump, you'll find that the flat surface of the wall helps line up Lara.

The series of jumps is very demanding. Be careful not to back up too far when you're making a run.

Pay particular attention to the headroom as you line up each leap. Think about where your arc will be its highest.

At the low area across the short gap, reverse and do a backflip. The following jump is of the running variety, though it looks short—you bang your head midway.

SECRET

In the Secret room, stand facing the first slope and jump to it. Keep jumping—three jumps and a grab—to reach the safe platform. Don't overlook the Shotgun Shells.

After retracing your path to the Quad Bike, make the big leap. Engage the brakes to power up the engine, and let 'er rip.

Hug the wall and coax the bike along whenever passing a dangerous drop-off.

SECRET

At the small pit, hop off the Quad and you can spy a ladder leading downward. A Secret lies below!

x

x

3

In order to continue with the Quad Bike past the sealed, gold-lattice door, you have to follow the hallways off the area with the big jump and open the door from the other side. It's a fairly straightforward exercise, except for the snakes lurking in the tunnel. Both of the blind corners with snakes are right-hand turns—one early on, the last where the hall appears to dead end up ahead.

Notice how you can back up to the wall, and the Quad lines up perfectly straight for each jump? How convenient.

Finally, circle to a high ledge—across a short, dark gap—and make an impressive leap for a distant ramp. Back up to the wall and get a full throttle run.

The Quad's path dead ends temporarily at a gold-lattice door. Disembark and check the wall near the ramp you just came from. Run and jump to the hallway.

Crawl along the path. When you stand, be wary of lurking snakes.

There are two cobras around blind corners in the short network of halls.

4

Once you make it through the gold-lattice door, the level path diverges at the Save Crystal. One route—the shortcut—takes off to the right, across the river. The main route is to the left. Once you go down the rocky path to the right, or across the wide jump to the left, you can't change your mind and go back again. This walkthrough continues at this point as if you wanted to test the shortcut first, realizing you'll probably want to start the level over and take the main route when the paths intersect later on. Remember, unless you have all the Secrets in the game, you can't reach the Secret Level.

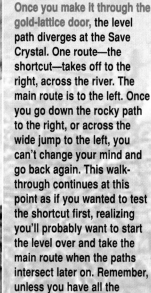

Jump from the edge of the hole to cross above the area where the Quad waits.

From the room with the second snake, drop down to the hallway. Expect malicious monkeys to intrude when you go near the door switch.

Atop the Quad once more, the area of the blue Save Crystal is where the paths in the level diverge. The right-hand route is the shortcut. The main trail is the only way to get all the Secrets.

Shortcut

Once you go to the right—the shortcut—the Quad rumbles down a blocky slope. There's no going back.

Jump the river, and don't be alarmed if the Quad goes down the hole in the ground. You were headed in that direction. If you wait down in the tunnel, a monkey will bring you a Small Medi Pack from up above.

5 The first of the two Gate Keys is relatively straightforward, resting in a small chamber in the vicinity of the greenish rocks—where the cave begins to look more like a temple. The crawlspace entrance to the temple halls is near the steep slope right before you get to those greenish rocks. Stand at the bottom of the slope, facing up it, and look to the right.

6

Get off the Quad and weed out the monkeys before continuing in the hallway.

The cave interior becomes brick and lattice, but that hallway is a dead end for now. On the green cliff nearby are two openings—low right and high left.

Check both chambers through the green wall; be ready for a lurking cobra.

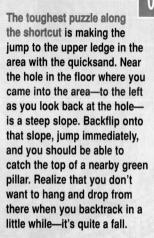

The toughest puzzle along the shortcut is making the jump to the upper ledge in the area with the quicksand. Near the hole in the floor where you came into the area—to the left as you look back at the hole—is a steep slope. Backflip onto that slope, jump immediately, and you should be able to catch the top of a nearby green pillar. Realize that you don't want to hang and drop from there when you backtrack in a little while—it's quite a fall.

Through the opening, high and left as you face the green wall, you can crawl to a small room with the first Gate Key. You'll need two such keys to proceed with the Quad Bike.

Along the steep section of the green tunnel, you should spy a crawlspace. That's the path forward.

Follow the hallways, wary of monkeys. At one point, you pass the ledges with the Gate Key locks.

Finally, you jump and grab a ledge at the end of a hallway and emerge in an open area. The ground near the gate is quicksand.

To continue from the open area with the Save Crystal—which you can reach easily—look back near the hole leading down to the hallway. Notice the steep slope.

Turn around like so, and backflip so that you land on the steep slope. Jump and grab immediately.

Bouncing off the steep slope, you should be able to grab the top of the tall green pillar. The hole down to the hallway is beneath you.

Jump across the branches to the opening in the wall.

From the branches of the tree on the far side of the wall, thin out the monkeys. Along the ledge to the right is the building's opening. To the left, you might leap ledges to an ammo stash.

7

The building holding the second Gate Key is a tame little excursion, with plenty of monkeys but little danger. When you go to backtrack, take time out to get the ammo from the high ledge, just inside the large gate that opens. You have to jump from the branches to one ledge, and from there to the ledge with the stash. Then again, you are going to restart this level …

On the top floor of the building, battle monkeys for the second Gate Key. Watch that flaming statue when you head downstairs.

Downstairs, the switch on the ledge opens the large gate in the outer area. Expect a multitude of monkeys to take notice of you.

Backtrack through the shortcut route to the ledge with locks. Now you can bring the Quad Bike up, and jump the quicksand mire.

8

This is the point where the shortcut path rejoins the main route—once you make the final jump across the river toward the Save Crystal. At that point, you're a few monkeys and some birds away from the end of the line. We'll cover the end of the level as part of the main route, and pick up the main route walkthrough from the place in the cave where the path diverges. The main route heads up a steep hill to the left. When it comes to jumping the gap in the hill, you needn't gun the engine to make it across, and very often that extra momentum is deadly. When you make it across the gap, hugging the right-hand wall, turn the Quad into the wall to arrest your momentum. Creep along until you make it safely past the large hole in the floor of the next room.

Main Route

Circle around the building which held the second Gate Key. You'll find a small jungle area back near the river. Check the slope you're jumping from for irregularities. When you cross back over the river, the shortcut path intersects with the main trail.

Back where the paths diverge, the left-hand route is the main trail, the path with all the Secret areas.

The long jump is a killer. Jump along the right-hand side of the slope and turn into the wall on the right, once you land, to arrest your momentum. Creep up the slope and through the door on the right.

Just through the right-hand door off the big slope there's a room with a big hole in the floor. Lovely.

Past the room with the hole in the floor, hug the right and stop at the top of the long, outside ramp. Climb off the Quad and go out onto the ramp. Look to the right and spy a Secret.

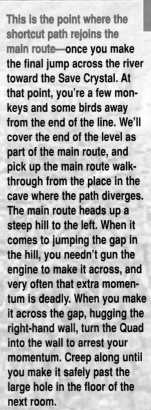

Once you take the Secret from the cliff wall, it's time to try the Quad out on the long ramp. Notice, near the top of the ramp, one surface you can stand on, and another that's a slope. For that reason, it seems like you're better off picking one side of the ramp or the other, instead of going right down the middle. The Quad can get squirrelly due to the difference in the gradient. We like the left. Brake, full throttle, and release. No need to worry about the landing.

SECRET

From the ledge with the ammo, jump up and grab the edge of the crawlspace. Don't overlook the Harpoons that Lara is standing on top of in this picture.

Secret in hand, get back on the Quad Bike. Pick one side of the ramp, instead of the middle. Back to the wall, engage the brake, gun the engine, and go!

Follow the hallway. It appears to split in two, but both routes are headed in the same general direction. Get off the bike and look around.

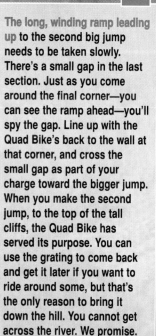

The long, winding ramp leading up to the second big jump needs to be taken slowly. There's a small gap in the last section. Just as you come around the final corner—you can see the ramp ahead—you'll spy the gap. Line up with the Quad Bike's back to the wall at that corner, and cross the small gap as part of your charge toward the bigger jump. When you make the second jump, to the top of the tall cliffs, the Quad Bike has served its purpose. You can use the grating to come back and get it later if you want to ride around some, but that's the only reason to bring it down the hill. You cannot get across the river. We promise.

The large hallways lead to an open area where you can see a Save Crystal far above. You'll have to jump the Quad Bike from an upper ramp on this side of the gorge.

The ramp is long but not too perilous, as long as you take it slowly.

Watch those corners. Notice how the Quad can almost pivot with the tiniest bit of forward momentum. Just past the final corner, where you can see the actual jump ahead, there's a hole in the ramp!

Back up flat against the wall with the hole in the ramp a few meters in front of you. Brakes! Throttle! Action!

In the area with the Save Crystal, you have one last big jump to look forward to. Hopefully those are getting to be routine. Climb down the ladder before you make the trip.

Across the last big jump, you sit atop a high cliff. The path to another Secret is along the ledge on the left. Expect a vulture to arrive as you descend the hill.

Follow the upper ledge near the tall cliff. Run and jump to a ledge across an impressive chasm.

11

The last bit of the level is really all about two Secrets. The first of the pair is the hardest to get without the standard screaming descent into oblivion. Use the screenshots as a guide. You have to hit the slope near the secret ledge so that you're sliding forward. This way, you can grab the ledge when you jump. Getting back to the path requires the same trick, though you don't have to grab a ledge on your return—just jump from the slope to the path.

SECRET

To make it to the ledge, you have to run and jump to the nearby slope, then jump quickly and grab the edge. Crawl inside for the Secret.

Getting back off the secret ledge is another jumping exercise. Jump to the slope, and jump again. You shouldn't have to grab.

12

Watch those birdies when you go to take the path near the waterfall. They'd really like you to fall into the pool below, and thus miss the final Secret of the level. That's why we opt for the Shotgun. One close-range blast is usually all it takes, and two *always* do the trick. You must bother with three of the big birds. Down the path, notice the tip-off ammo stash which lets you know where to make that last jump. Once you have the last Secret, drop down to the water and pass through the waterfall to exit.

There really is no reason to go back for the Quad Bike, if you left it behind. If you'd like to go get it for grins, this is your last chance. The area up ahead is where the main route intersects the shortcut.

From the platform above the falls, you can see the final secret—the dirty ledge low and to the right.

When you jump to the short ledge to climb the cliffs opposite the falls, a trio of buzzards attacks. Put your back to the wall and whip out the Shotgun.

From a lower ledge facing the cliff face with the secret entrance, look down and spy some ammo.

From the area of the ammo, you can plainly see a long crack leading to the secret.

Run, jump, and grab from the area of the ammo to catch the ledge. Shimmy right.

The River Ganges is demanding, but relatively quick. Hopefully you can conserve some Save Crystals.

Pass through the waterfall and climb the rocks to the tunnel exit.

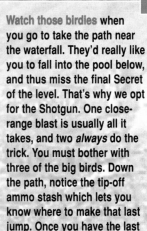

India

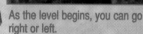

Jungle

Temple Ruins

The River Ganges

Caves of Kaliya

SECRET

0 secrets

The maddening little maze of Kaliya is a tedious test, mainly due to the fact that it's easy to wander off looking for ammo, and suddenly all those intersections look pretty much the same. Fortunately, there's no great need to scour the tunnels for treasures: there's not a lot to speak of. The walkthrough, then, is a fairly straight-forward path to the showdown. We used Flares to help light the intersections and to highlight specific entryways and passages. If you've already been lost awhile, it's probably best to just restart the level and take it from the top. The good news is it's a quick trip.

1

2

As the level begins, you can go right or left.

To the left lies nothing but Flares. Might as well go get 'em.

At the intersection, there are two dead ends to the right, a crawl space to the near left …

… and a long hall to the left of the crawlspace.

Of course, you can always find a snake to kill. It's not nearly satisfying enough to warrant the trouble.

If you follow the hallway to the left from the intersection, you round the corner to find a hole in the floor.

Drop down through the hole. At the bottom of the area, you'll find a pack of Flares (See box 2).

Double back to the beginning of the level. This time, choose the right-hand path.

Crawl through to a spot above a long ramp. A boulder will follow you down.

About 15 meters from the bottom of the ramp, jump. You don't want to jump from so high that Lara falls into a crouch. You can sprint a tiny bit if you want.

The pair of early boulder traps is just about all the level has to offer in the way of obstacles. The first boulder drops onto the long slope as you slide toward the hallway below. You can get a bit of an edge, speed-wise, if you jump the last small portion of the ramp. Don't jump from too high up, or your landing won't be a smooth, running transition. As long as Lara doesn't fall into the kneeling position momentarily on impact, you'll have just enough time to make it down the long hall and dodge to either side at the intersection. You can sprint a short portion of the hall, but don't do it for very long: traveling at high speed, it can be tough making the turn in the intersection.

At the bottom of the ramp, you have to make a quick left to avoid the boulder (See box 3).

From the point where the boulder stops, a hallway leads off to the left.

Down the hallway there's a niche on the right. You'll need to use that to escape from the path of the next boulder. Throw a Flare into the niche.

Run down the hallway about 10 meters and roll. If the boulder drops, run back down the hall. If it doesn't, venture a bit farther and roll again.

When the boulder drops, beat feet back to the lit niche.

The second boulder is a tough one since it leaves you very little time to react. From the place where the first boulder stops, the hallway leads to the left. That's where the second boulder is. The niche on the right is the safe spot you run for when the rock drops. Throw a Flare into the niche. Go past the niche about 10 or so meters and roll. Run back down the hallway. If you don't hear the boulder, it ain't comin'. Go back down toward the boulder, and go a little farther, then roll again. Rinse and repeat. If the Flare goes out while you're inching up the hall, relight it. It helps to see the turn when the boulder is right behind you.

You should have enough time to avoid the second boulder and reach safety. Once it passes, continue down the hallway (See box 4).

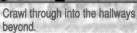

At the end of the hallway, there's a ledge you can jump up and grab.

Crawl through into the hallways beyond.

To the left, cautiously make a wide turn around the corner.

Pause to take out the snake. There are others you can hunt, if you so desire.

To the right from the crawlspace entrance is the correct route (See box 5).

At the intersection—which you'll soon double back to, take a right.

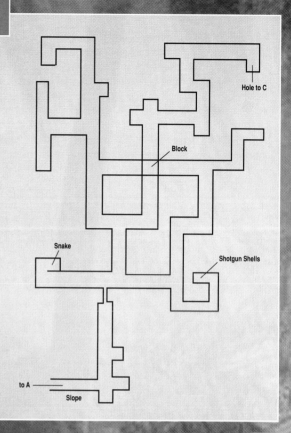

5

Hole to C

Block

Snake

Shotgun Shells

to A

Slope

Follow the hallway as it winds to the left.

Grab the Shotgun shells. Now double back to that last intersection (See box 5).

Back at the intersection, the crawl space entrance is to the left. Head to the right.

Follow the hallway.

6

In the area of the caves that returns to the temple motif, the passages interlace around a movable block. There are a couple of different ways to get through the area—due to your ability to reposition the block. Taking the path here is expedient. Snake kills are optional. The motif starts to turn back to the mossy, underground look once you get near the hole in the tunnel floor: that's the big tip-off that you're headed in the right direction.

At the slightly raised floor in the intersection, look to the left.

Push the block at the end of the short hall past the raised floor.

From the point where you push the block, turn and head to the right.

Head to the right at the next intersection.

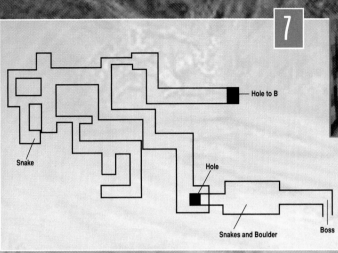

Follow the hallway. There are several short dead ends, but only one long hall.

At the end of the long hall you'll find a hole in the floor.

Drop down the hole and continue to follow the hall.

Climb up the ledge and crawl through the crawlspace to the intersection.

The path to the lair is to the left, just out of the crawl space.

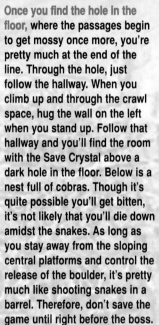

Once you find the hole in the floor, where the passages begin to get mossy once more, you're pretty much at the end of the line. Through the hole, just follow the hallway. When you climb up and through the crawl space, hug the wall on the left when you stand up. Follow that hallway and you'll find the room with the Save Crystal above a dark hole in the floor. Below is a nest full of cobras. Though it's quite possible you'll get bitten, it's not likely that you'll die down amidst the snakes. As long as you stay away from the sloping central platforms and control the release of the boulder, it's pretty much like shooting snakes in a barrel. Therefore, don't save the game until right before the boss.

Follow the hallway from the intersection, and you'll find a room with a Save Crystal above a hole in the floor. Take the Flares, and jump over the hole to take the crystal.

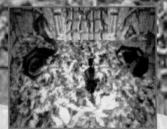

Hang and drop down the hole and you'll land in the middle of four snakes.

Step back onto the plant in the middle of the floor and you're in a safe zone.

Dispose of the snakes in that half of the room and notice the two ramps.

When you go near the ramps, a boulder rolls through the room. You can use the ramps to leap above the boulder, but the nearby cobras usually tag you in the process.

You can use the ramps in the snake room as springboards and bounce back and forth above the boulder as it rolls through the room, but that turns out to be a little too tricky. The cobras on the far side of the ramp get to take bites at you as you bounce. Draw out the boulder by walking carefully out between the slopes and then backing quickly away when you hear the boulder. Then you can enter the second half of the snake chamber and take care of the rest of the crew.

The showdown can be rough, unless of course you know what we're about to divulge. The caveat: This works about 80 percent of the time, so you should certainly save the game before fighting the boss. The floor of the lair is mostly toxic, and the firebolts which are the fiend's favorite mode of attack have a homing ability. If you can kill him this way, it takes about 30 seconds. As you slide into the room, tap the Look button to get Lara's eyes off the freak's transformation and break to the left. Run and jump to the platform there and run down the length of the platform near the wall. Stop in the sector which sticks out from the far end of the platform near the wall. Turn toward the boss in the center of the chamber and square up, so that Lara's back is flat against the wall behind her. Draw your Pistols. By jumping right and left—twice in each direction—you can evade the boss's blasts while keeping up a withering assault of your own. Don't freak out if you jump straight up in the air occasionally: sometimes it's a good thing to vary the rhythm. Occasionally, the badguy wins. There's just no way to always avoid a homing missile. But moving at all times is a really good start. Oh, and don't even think about going for the Grenade Launcher first. Even if you get it, it seems to have no effect ....

Step toward the flat area between the ramps. When you hear the boulder start rolling, simply step back to one side.

The boulder rolls through and off down a long hallway.

In the second section of the room there are six more snakes to slay.

Follow the hallway where the boulder made its exit and crawl through the space. Collect the Save Crystal and Small Medi Pack.

Save the game before sliding down the ramp.

The boss makes quite a display upon your arrival. The water becomes lethal.

The platform to the left of the entry ramp makes a good place to jump back and forth.

The extended edge of the ramp means that you can jump twice in either direction—back and forth—while chipping away.

When the boss goes out he goes out in style.

Run and jump around to the platforms, collecting the Grenade Launcher and refills. When you take the relic from the central section, the level ends.

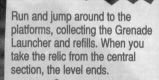

India

Nevada

Nevada Desert

High Security Compund

Area 51

SECRET 3 secrets

The Nevada Desert concerns itself primarily with the area in and around a huge canyon. No biggy, except that you tend to spend roughly a zillion hours trying to find a shortcut through that chunk of the level, when you should just be biting the bullet and backtracking. The backtracking isn't even that bad— maybe seven jumps—but the vastness of the canyon gets you thinking it's a long haul. Not really. Stop wasting time. The first part of the level is the quick trip to the canyon: watch out for irregular ledges and snakes in the bushes.

Look to the skies as the level gets underway, and get used to it. You never know what you might see …

There's also rattlers to contend with. They favor the bushes. Off to the right, a snake rests with a rocket.

Cross the pool and explore the passage. There's a hallway at the far end that's hard to see from a distance.

Push the movable block that you find along the path. Take the ammo and continue up the trail.

The first Secret is a bit of a doozy, since the key is the movable box: unless you push it and leave it alone, you get stuck in the secret chamber. Swell. Push the box and jump down into the chamber at a very specific spot from the platform. The jumps on either side of the platform are the run, jump, and grab variety: if you try to just stand and leap, you wind up in the barbwire below.

From the central platform of the two running jumps, you can hang and drop into a barbwire-free zone.

SECRET

Take the goodies from the snakes (See box 2). Remember the barbwire behind you.

To exit the area, you push the block that you pushed just a few moments before (See box 2). Dealing with the nearby snake *first* is prudent.

Continue along the path, perhaps walking slowly to the right of the metal box, ready to pan the camera up and to the right …

Run and jump from the trail near the metal box to the ledge.

Dispose of the snake near the bush, then run and jump to the closest portion of the distant walkway.

NEVADA DESERT

To get into the canyon, you must first get into the large metal box, which is actually a chute to a waterway below. Follow the cliffs around and leap to the front of the rock formation. Once you make the canyon, you'll probably want to save your game. Consider, however, that there's very little that can actually kill you here: any fall is broken by the water below. No, go ahead and save …

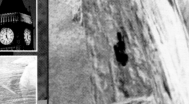

Run off the end of the path when it dead-ends, and you'll land on a ledge below.

Continue along the trail, stepping down to claim a Large Medi Pack, then go back to the trail and run for the rocks.

Run, jump, and grab toward the rock pile from the ledge, and continue to the top of the box, wary of the snake.

As we mentioned earlier, don't be put off by the dimensions of the canyon. You have to make the trip a grand total of three times. It takes about three minutes each time. The trickiest part of backtracking is the leap from the tall, reddish pillar to the slope across the canyon. If you try to grab the slope, the trajectory of your jump lowers, and you come up short. Simply run and jump to the slope and Lara will actually land on her feet. The trick to getting at the secret ledge is hanging on the extreme right when you drop to the crack nearby. That way, Lara will go into shimmy mode, instead of doing the climb pose on the entire surface.

Drop through the hole in the top of the large metal box and you'll fall into a waterway far below. Swim along until you can surface.

The large canyon is dominated by the waterfalls at one end.

In the opposite direction from the falls, the trail is less glamorous. That's your route. Be ready for a bird attack the first time down the path.

There are a couple of harrowing jumps—like around a corner to grab a ledge—but get used to it. This is the big backtrack route.

Eventually, you reach a high ledge. You should be on the same level with the rock formation.

Run and jump across the canyon to the ledge on the far side. Since this is your first trip, you might as well climb down and get the secret.

Move to the far right-hand side of the ladder, then drop and grab the ledge below. Immediately shimmy to the right.

SECRET

From the Secret, you have no choice but to jump into the canyon, but that's a good thing. There's a ton of ammo on the river floor. Time for that first backtrack. Getting to the ledge with the Save Crystal is a bit of a test. Don't try to force anything. Make the obvious jumps—and the one monkeybars bit—and refer to the screens if you get hung up. The big thing is noticing the crack below you as you get very near the ledge.

Climb onto the ledge. The hard part is the drop to the crack: doing it so that you shimmy, as opposed to sticking to the ladder.

From the Secret, drop into the water below. There's plenty of stuff scattered on the river floor. Don't overlook the waterfall niches.

From the water, climb the low red rock near the waterfall. Climb the tall red rock next to that. Run and jump to the slope directly across the canyon. Don't grab! If you grab, you fall low of the mark. If you just run and jump, you arrive standing up.

Time for the big backtrack numero uno. Head back around the canyon as you did to find the secret, but this time stick to the upper path.

Jump shy of the bush, or you'll step on the snake lurking thereabouts.

On the ledge with the Save Crystal, you'll find the huge box of TNT. Your primary task is to detonate it. This is certainly an optimum point at which to save your progress. Two of the three canyon trips are behind you, and a harrowing series of leaps up the waterfall are just ahead.

Don't fall in the hole on the ledge when you jump past the rock.

Past the rock and the hole, hang from the ledge and drop to the crack below. Shimmy left.

From the ledge at the end of the crack, jump up and grab the underside of the ledge.

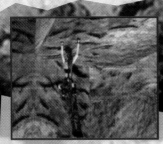

Swing hand-over-hand to the cliff face. Press up against the cliff, then drop and grab to hold the surface. Climb to the left and up.

In the area near the Save Crystal, you can see a big TNT box down below. There are also Flares down there. You need the Detonator Key to set off the charge. Now's a good time to save.

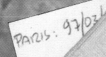
PARIS: 97/03/

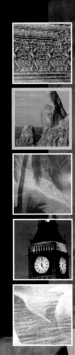

The trip up the falls is demanding. You first have to get the nerve to backflip off of the tall ladder, and then jump to a a slope in order to clear the chasm. If you just jump and grab the edge of the slope, instead of holding down the Forward key the whole time, you'll hang serenely from the side of the rock. Pull up when you're ready to take the big leap. Don't jump instantly: try to jump about halfway down the slope.

Jump to the slope beside the falls, and grab the edge when you slide.

Climb down to the ledge below, Follow it along the cliff.

From the end of the ledge, jump and grab the tall climbable surface. Climb all the way to the top, and backflip to a flat rock.

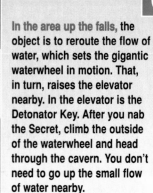

In the area up the falls, the object is to reroute the flow of water, which sets the gigantic waterwheel in motion. That, in turn, raises the elevator nearby. In the elevator is the Detonator Key. After you nab the Secret, climb the outside of the waterwheel and head through the cavern. You don't need to go up the small flow of water nearby.

From the flat rock, jump and grab the slope in between the falls. When you pull up, you'll slide toward a ledge. Jump and grab.

Take the ammo, jump to the crack, and shimmy right. When the camera pulls back, drop and jump to backflip across the waterway.

Jump the small platforms up the stream. A gigantic waterwheel dominates the cavern.

On the left shore, round a boulder to the left and kill a snake. About-face at that point and crawl under the large rock.

SECRET

Up the ladder, exit by climbing to the left and dropping to the floor. If you backflip blindly, Lara will land on a snake.

Back on the shore, there's a small chamber to the left of the waterwheel. Inside is an elevator in the down position. On the elevator is the Detonator Key for the TNT.

Kill the badguy and climb the waterwheel.

To start the waterwheel, you first have to throw the underwater switch near the falls. Remember to get the ammo in the underwater chamber before you divert the flow. Swim into the tunnel that opens and look up quickly to see the large dark texture above the tunnel. Pull that switch. Now swim through the tunnel, pulling another switch along the way, and you can access the hallway. Grab the goodies from the dry river bed before backtracking.

Follow the sides of the channel to an open area, ready for an air assault. In the water to the right, which is safe, you can swim down to a switch which opens a nearby door.

Once you collect the ammo from the small underwater chamber, throw the switch closer to the falling water.

As soon as you go inside the underwater tunnel that opens, look for a switch on the dark wall overhead. Pull it.

Swim through the tunnel, pulling another more obvious switch, and you'll surface in a hallway. Throwing the switch here activates the waterwheel.

On your way back to the waterwheel, check the dry river bed. You can jump to the upper ledge, then back to the river bed. There's a block below that let's you get behind the falls. You can get back to the river bed from one end of that same block.

Backtrack to the TNT box and blow open the cave to reach the new area. You did get those Flares first, didn't you? Watch the electrified fence as you explore: one touch means a grim, pyrotechnic death. Follow along with the screens. You're in the home stretch now.

Your ultimate destination is the elevator chamber near the waterwheel.

Dispose of the guard and take the Detonator. Now it's time to backtrack once again.

Back at the TNT box, notice the boulder that will threaten to ruin the big moment. Use the Detonator and jump to the left.

In the blown-up area, climb the ledges. From the highest, large ledge, you can climb to the next area.

It's a quick trip around this large area, if you know where you're going. Circle the fence to the left and climb to the narrow, dark passage.

NEVADA DESERT

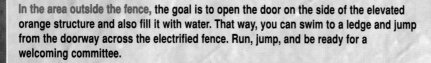

11

In the area outside the fence, the goal is to open the door on the side of the elevated orange structure and also fill it with water. That way, you can swim to a ledge and jump from the doorway across the electrified fence. Run, jump, and be ready for a welcoming committee.

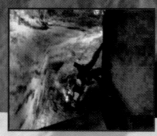

At the juncture, jump and grab the upper ledge. There's no need to go down just yet.

Swim down in the chamber: there are two switches to pull. One is behind the pillar, the other is in the tunnel.

Backtrack to the area near the electrified fence. This time, go down the wide cave opening.

12

Once you realize that someone left the Generator Access Pass on top of one of the buildings, things fall into place. Kill the guys, use the pass, open the fence. Riding the Quad Bike up the ramp is not advisable: you're likely to scoot off the far side, and perhaps into the fence. Get up a good head of steam and use the Quad Bike to jump the fence down in the cave. You're outta here ...

Snuff the snakes and throw the switch inside the small building.

Return to the narrower passage, and choose the low road at the juncture. Once the guards are dealt with, you can jump from the structure to a box across the fence.

Expect trouble as soon as you hit the box across the fence. Remember that nearby lethal current as you fight: best to get out of the narrow area.

In the buildings you'll find bad guys, a lock, and the Quad Bike.

You can ride the Quad to the top of the building (risky) or use the box and grating to climb to the Generator Access Pass roof.

Backflip when you open the generator room and take decisive action.

With the electricity off, open up the main gate—the switch is right beside it. Ride the Quad Bike down into the cave and use the big jump to clear the fence.

Nevada

Nevada Desert

High Security Compound

Area 51

SECRET

2 secrets

Time to bite the big bullet. You arrive at the High Security Compound with little more than lint in your pockets. Pretty much everything is gone, with the exception of Save Crystals. Lean on your ability to save the game, then feel secure in the knowledge that there are more Save Crystals up ahead (and a ton in Area 51). Also, as you'll soon realize, the inmates are Lara's friends. Use them to battle the military goons. Just lead the offending party to the prisoners' area and let nature take its course. Don't miss that first Secret. One major backtrack is enough, and the second Secret is one of the toughest finds in the whole game.

Jump into the window to summon the guard. When he arrives, sprint past him and off the railing outside.

Wait for the guard to chase you down the stairs, then hustle back up toward your cell.

Hit the switch on the wall beside the cell next door, and the inmate comes out to battle the guard.

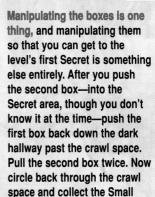

Manipulating the boxes is one thing, and manipulating them so that you can get to the level's first Secret is something else entirely. After you push the second box—into the Secret area, though you don't know it at the time—push the first box back down the dark hallway past the crawl space. Pull the second box twice. Now circle back through the crawl space and collect the Small Medi Pack. What, no Uzis?

Open up all the cell doors, and notice the one which was open to begin with.

Inside the previously opened cell, a box sits in a passage.

Push the first box, and a crawl space is revealed.

SECRET

Crawl through, and push the box, this allows you to push the first box back down the passage, exposing the same crawl space, now on your right.

By manipulating the boxes and using the crawl space, you can reach the sector that you originally pushed the second box into (See box 2).

Up above the passage which leads from the cell, you can jump and grab a walkway.

Run and jump across the barbwire pit.

NEVADA DESERT

3

Getting into the main complex requires you to negotiate some dark corridors. When you first climb down through the trapdoor, look for the ledge on the left. You can't survive the trip to the bottom of the ladder. Jump that first trapdoor in the hallway or you'll drop into an area far from the switch that releases the inmates, and very close to an MP. Not good.

Walk through the barbwire to reach the switch.

Use the ledge near the switch to reach the trapdoor. Climb about halfway down and look for a ledge on the left.

Jump over the first trapdoor you come across in the darkened hallway.

4

Getting to the area behind the wire mesh in the kitchen is the next big test. You first have to move the big box around its little path, and then turn off the grill in the kitchen. The route itself isn't too tricky: watch your step and all's well.

Drop through the trapdoor in the small room and you'll fall into a control center. Hit the button on the wall nearby.

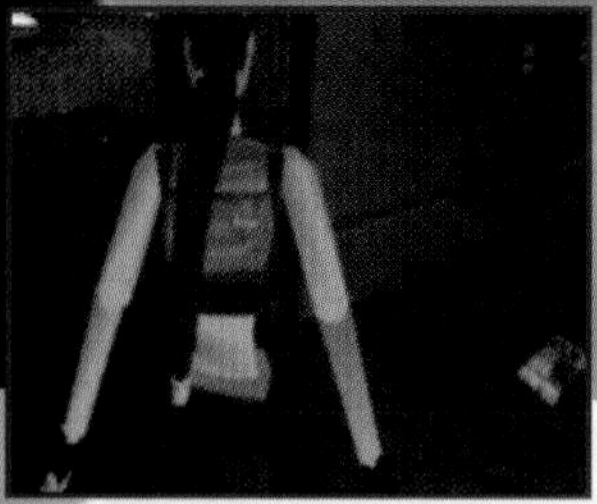

The inmates arrive to mug the MP, who drops a Security Pass.

Check the door to the left of the dining room entrance.

The room with the large boxes is a straightforward movement puzzle.

Run around the room, pushing the movable box beneath the hole in the ceiling.

Up above the box room, jump the pipe and throw the switch on the wall.

Swim back through the box room, and up through another hole in the ceiling.

Once you make it into the kitchen, you need only make your exit in the proper fashion. In the small hallway off the kitchen are two doors. Round the corner, open the door on the right, then come back to the first door. That way, when the bad guys come out to punish you, there's somewhere to run. Head back through the kitchen, hang a right and then a quick left. The cell block is up ahead.

Jump across the sizzling kitchen to the room with the red floor.

Follow the walkway, wary of barbwire pits.

In the yellow chamber, throw the switch on the wall to shut off the kitchen grill.

Backtrack through the hole in the ceiling where you arrive—though the button opens the nearby door.

Double back to the outer walkway, and then go through the room with the red floor to the hole above the kitchen.

The switch that opens the mesh near the fans is in the room that the guard came running out of. Slide and jump to the crack, then shimmy left. Drop and jump and you'll land on safe ground. Follow the corridor through the crawl space, and don't sweat the inmate up above.

Drop down into the kitchen and open the door at the far end.

In the short hallway, open the door around the corner to the right before you open the portal on the left.

Sprint back through the kitchen and buttonhook right, then turn left in the hallway. You have to beat feet back to the cell block so that the inmates can help you.

Check the room that the guard came out of to find the switch that raises the vent above the kitchen grill.

Jump to the crack and shimmy left, then jump from the sloped surface to the flat area across the pit. Climb up into the crawl space.

NEVADA DESERT

The trick to making it past the guard at the top of the green hallway is to let him pass to the left. Sprint across the area to the right before he reverses in the dark hallway. Now you're home free. The inmate you release down below will go back to that guard and pummel him out of a Security Pass.

Follow the passage. The man in the corridor is an inmate.

In the steep green hallway, let the guard pass. Now sprint up.

Hang a right and hustle across the large area. Don't let the guard see you.

Of course, the prisoners are doing most of the work for you here. Ah, sweet revenge. Getting past the guard near the switched door requires some stealth. Crawl over and try to throw the switch when the guard is to the left (as you stand facing the switch). A deadly beam cuts across the room at the same time the door opens, and it's best if the guard is on that side of the laser. Jump the beam and bolt through the open door: the guard may get off a couple of shots.

Follow the open passage to the lower cell block.

When you open the cell door, the inmate hustles up the corridor. Follow him.

Up above, you'll see that the inmate has taken care of business. Pick up the Security Pass and use it on the nearby door.

Follow the large passage once you've deactivated the electric beams. Get the guard's attention, then run left down the hallway.

Open the cell in the corridor and take the key that the guard drops. It fits in the lock in the large open area.

When you see the guard below, crouch down and go through the crawl space.

Crawl over to the switch. The guard is armed. Hit the switch when the guard is on your left (as you face the switch) and jump the red electric beam to enter the hallway (See box 8).

The area around the big dish is demanding, mainly because you can never quite be sure where you should go. There's also the matter of the big backtrack for the level's final Secret. Be mindful that you don't inadvertently close the door that you'll want to have open later. Also, notice the Secret area the first time you're there. You'll have to come back once you've found the Pistols in order to claim the prize.

Follow the hall to the large chamber. Along the walkway, look down and spy an opening just above a platform. Moving the big dish is not such a big deal.

Instead of jumping through the hole beneath the big dish, hang and drop from the lowest support to the ground far below. Ouch!

Climb the ladder off of the ground level.

In the corridor, sneak past the guard. Remember this spot. Later on there's a Secret nearby.

Backtrack with the Security Pass to the red hallway.

The door that you want to open—and not close up afterwards—is the one near the grated wall in the small yellowish alcove. It has a little half-window you can peek through. An underwater tunnel off of the large pool beneath the big dish allows you to backtrack. Don't go into the hallway when you first open it, as there's a guard on patrol.

Put the Security Pass in the lock and climb the ladder.

Near the door, push the button to open the portal. The switch on the other side of the grating will close the door up again: *do not* go to the trouble of finding that switch. It's evil.

The hole in the side of the large chamber, above the waterline, is the path to the evil switch. Don't do it. Jump in the water and take the Save Crystal as you swim down the tunnel.

Swim the long tunnel and then backtrack for the power-ups. In the small room, be mindful not to surface in the path of the electric beams. Climb up and jump the beams to the ledge.

In the cargo area, climb the boxes on the left. **Pistols** and the **Desert Eagle** await you in the small room.

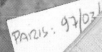

PARIS: 97/03

NEVADA DESERT

Getting the Pistols and the Desert Eagle is the easy part. The turret waiting when you exit just about cuts poor Lara in half. Sprint out the door, hang a right, and you can reach the safety of the over-hanging ledge. When you reemerge, the gun will have reset and you can climb the boxes free from harm. Getting back to the Secret is a trek. The key to success is having opened the door beforehand, as we have belabored. It's also important that you *did not* reseal the door by reaching the switch on the other side of the grating. Bypass that whole business entirely. In the large pool, look for the corridor—it's low and in one corner. If you get sucked off to one side, swim back toward the center of the chamber and then turn toward the corridor.

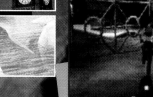

When you exit the room, sprint through the electric eye and beneath the ledge as the gun turret unloads. The gun will reset once you're out of sight. Climb the boxes back to the cargo area.

Time for the big Secret backtrack. Since the door in the yellowish alcove is open, you can make it back to the floor area of the chamber with the big dish.

Go all the way back to the guard that was looking in the wrong direction. He's armed and dangerous. Take the Security Pass he drops and open the door at the far end of the corridor.

The final bit of the level is a major shoot-em-up, as military muscle men come crawling out of the woodwork. Try to use the Pistols as much as possible, only resorting to the Desert Eagle when an opponent is armed. Even then, if you can be mobile and conserve your ammo, do it. You only have to make it to the end of the game, and Lara can get healthy on the truck ride to Area 51.

In the short hallway, pick up the **Grenade Launcher**.

Backtrack once more—all the way to the cargo room. Head up the wide slope, ready for armed resistance.

Clear the hallway and take the ladder upstairs.

The button on the right is the one you want in order to move the boxes. The other lets enemies enter from the nearby gate.

Use the box to climb to the upper ledge in the cargo area.

Monkey-swing over to the ledge. Watch that winch when you exit back to this area— that's when it's a killer. Kill the guard above and take his Security Pass.

Open the final locked gate and rid the area of villains. When you climb into the back of the truck, the level ends.

Nevada

Nevada Desert

High Security Compound

Area 51

The big trick to Area 51 is realizing that half the people who see you aren't attacking, they're going for an alarm pad. Stop them. You just can't afford to have the added heat the alarm brings, as well as the fact that several times it costs you valuable prizes. The first instance is right out of the truck. If you don't run down that first guy, it's time to reload: the MP5 is out of reach. Also, get in the habit of searching the MPs. Every once in a while, they cough up a Small Medi Pack or ammo, but the items can be hard to see due to their dark uniforms.

Exit the truck and pillage the boxes on the left, then give chase to the guard. You can't let him reach the distant alarm.

As long as the guard doesn't reach the alarm pad, the **MP5** is within your reach. Leave the switch alone.

Use the nearby button to open the grating and crawl through. Take the Large Medi Pack.

Get used to the timing of the rolling laser trap: **it's a recur**ring theme. In the first instance, be sure you're holding down the Crouch button when you crawl into the corridor. Crawl toward the thing from the low point in the floor and you can crawl into the space with the Large Medi Pack. Crawl back out again, then stand and run for the ladder as soon as the trap moves behind you. When you come to the guard pacing outside the crawl space, inch forward until he appears. Let him pass to the right, then crawl out. Plug him with the Desert Eagle from a distance before he turns around.

As you enter the dangerous crawl space, crouch and crawl to the left. You have to time it just right, but it's worth another Large Medi Pack.

Crawl back into the laser tunnel as the trap moves away. When it passes overhead, stand and run to the ledge, using the Action and Forward buttons to climb up quickly.

Wait for the guard to pass on your right, and crawl quickly out of the crawl space.

You have to stop the guard before he gets to the alarm pad. Try the Desert Eagle. Expect more trouble when you open the room nearby.

Crawl through the hole in the wall to avoid the laser-trigger turret up ahead. Follow the hallway.

Take out the guard in the long hallway. Round the corner to the switch above the obvious trapdoor.

Throw the switch and let Lara fall. There's no need to be too tricky.

NEVADA DESERT

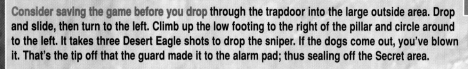

Consider saving the game before you drop through the trapdoor into the large outside area. Drop and slide, then turn to the left. Climb up the low footing to the right of the pillar and circle around to the left. It takes three Desert Eagle shots to drop the sniper. If the dogs come out, you've blown it. That's the tip off that the guard made it to the alarm pad; thus sealing off the Secret area.

From where Lara lands, turn to the left and go around to the right of the pillar. When you step around the pillar, look to the left. A guard will be going for an alarm pad. If he makes it, he seals off a Secret and let's loose some doggies. Go with the Eagle.

Once you've collected the Grenades, drop down to the wire mesh floor and pull the switch.

A trapdoor drops you to the area below. Kill the guard on duty. If you stopped the sniper upstairs, the grating is open.

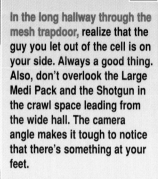

In the long hallway through the mesh trapdoor, realize that the guy you let out of the cell is on your side. Always a good thing. Also, don't overlook the Large Medi Pack and the Shotgun in the crawl space leading from the wide hall. The camera angle makes it tough to notice that there's something at your feet.

SECRET

As long as the sniper in the upper area was killed before reaching the alarm pad, the small crawl space is open.

Collect the ammo and drop through the trapdoor mesh to the hallway below. Deal with the guard and investigate the corner nearby.

When you open the small cell with the switch in the hall, the prisoner you let loose takes on the arriving MP. Crawl in and get the Large Medi Pak.

In the long hallway, bypass the laser traps in favor of the crawl space. On the way to the adjoining hall, you'll pick up another Large Medi Pak, and the **Shotgun**.

Kill the MP. The buttons on the large panels are monitors for the trap up ahead.

Time to field test the ol' MP5. When you go for the door in the chamber, bad guys arrive from either side.

A switch in one bad guy's alcove opens the crawl space in the other.

Best to whip out the heavy artillery for the trio of thugs near the orange portal off the lower hallway. Conversely, you can take the sniper who holds the Code Clearance Disk and your Pistols, as long as you jump back and forth from behind the wall. You can get at the Secret earlier if you go through the grating—from the floor as opposed to the ledge above. It's just that those winch things are nasty, and why dodge past one if you don't have to?

Trip the green alarm beams and shoot the guard. Continue up the corridor.

When the corridor branches, head to the right.

Use the cover of the wall to take down the sniper near the rocket. Take the Code Clearance Disk from the ledge and return to the hallway through which you arrived.

At the other end of the hallway—the left turn from the steep corridor—is the console which requires the disk. Hop over the intersecting alarm beams.

With the missile lifted, you can reach the ammo on the ledge. Yes, there's a Secret place nearby. Patience.

To get to the sniper in the upper area—the one that drops the Hangar Access Key—use the arc of the ceiling beams. You need to use the arcs so that Lara doesn't bang her pretty head at the apex of the jump. When you jump off of the ledge near the winch, after getting the Secret Save Crystal, don't forget about the trigger beams down below.

Run and jump to the ladder between the two missiles. Backflip from the top of the climb.

Peg the sniper in the far corner of the upper area with the Desert Eagle. Leap to the sniper's ledge, using the gap in the beams above, and take the Hangar Access Key.

At the other end of the sniper's ledge, drop down to the platform on the other side of the winch.

SECRET

Shoot the funky grating on the wall near the winch and climb into the tunnel. Follow the corridor for your prize.

Head back to the rocket room. There's a hallway at floor level.

NEVADA DESERT

Use extreme caution near the train, as the rail is deadly. You have to climb up the mesh grating at one end of the tunnel—the safe end—to summon the tram. When you do the monkey swing, you'll hear the grates opening up beneath you. Watch where the laser trap reverses and move up just shy of that point. When the trap rolls away, swing after it. Jump down when it reverses back toward you.

Past the monkey swing, run and jump to the platform across the way, ready to unload some ammo. Don't grab for the ledge, or you'll come up short. Stop the cop before he runs off, and reload with those shells near the train rail. Past the saucer, the large room with the two switches is tough. Give each button a test push and kill the snipers which appear below. Stand and face the buttons. Push the left-hand one first. Jump right and roll to make it quickly to the end of the walk, then use the white top of the control center to run across to the other walkway. When you hop down to run for the door, don't bring Lara to her knees with a big jump. That's a really irritating reason for missing the puzzle.

Step past the hole in the floor. That's launch control. Continue in the upper hallway and apply the Hangar Access Key to the lock.

Kill the guard on the train platform and drop carefully into the area near the electrified rail. Climb the mesh and push the button.

The train arrives far down the track when you push the button. From the nearby ledge, stand and jump to the corner of the car.

From the end of the train, jump up and grab the edge of the hallway above.

Jump up and use the monkey swing above the second set of gratings. You'll have to follow the laser trap for a short distance, then turn and drop to solid ground when the trap approaches.

Run and jump to the platform and whip out that Shotgun to deal with the fleeing figure. If he makes it off up the hallway, many more enemies will lie in wait.

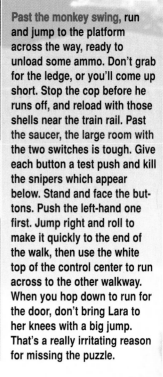

Follow the hallway around the UFO. Be careful not to trip any of the green electric eyes, or the gun turrets make you pay.

Climb the boxes to the opposite hall, mindful of another guard up ahead. He breaks left to right in the large room, going for an alarm down the short hallway.

The first time you push each of the buttons on the upper walk, a sniper appears in the hallway below. Take care of them before trying the puzzle for real.

As you face the buttons, push the left one first, then the right. Use the white top of the console to move quickly from one ledge to the other, and also to cushion your jump to the floor.

When you launch the rocket with the key from atop the saucer, you have zero time to enjoy the lift-off. Jump left, roll, and run. Once you start running, sprint. Keep on going to the far end of the room that opens as flames boil behind you. Once the rocket's gone, you can climb high up into that chamber, snagging a Large Medi Pack on the way up.

Relieve the guard and flip the switches. Try the two on the right end, then try the switch that's one in from the left-hand side. When activated simultaneously, the UFO becomes accessible.

Back near the UFO, push the button and climb the ladder. Backflip from the top of the ladder to the rafters.

Run and jump around the rafters. You can step down to a walkway above the saucer. Later on, you'll have to repeat the rafter walk to get the nearby Secret. Not yet.

Backtrack. The Launch Code from the top of the saucer goes in a key reader down the hole in the floor. Now you're at Launch Control, back near the big rocket room.

The key from the top of the saucer makes the button accessible. When you push the button, jump left, roll, and run into a full sprint. Keep running straight while the cinematic plays.

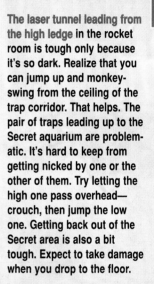

The laser tunnel leading from the high ledge in the rocket room is tough only because it's so dark. Realize that you can jump up and monkey-swing from the ceiling of the trap corridor. That helps. The pair of traps leading up to the Secret aquarium are problematic. It's hard to keep from getting nicked by one or the other of them. Try letting the high one pass overhead—crouch, then jump the low one. Getting back out of the Secret area is also a bit tough. Expect to take damage when you drop to the floor.

Climb high up in the area where the rocket was launched. Kill the guard and open the nearby corridor. It'll seal behind you.

Past the laser trap, plug the sniper. Rid the general area of villains and collect the key which accesses the saucer. Throw the switch downstairs to open the trapdoor.

Backtrack to the saucer area. Take the goodies from the area and climb back into the rafters. Past the walkway leading out to the saucer, run, jump, and grab to the open doorway.

SECRET

From the upper rafters, you can enter a hallway connecting to the huge aquarium. Take the Save Crystal and don't fool around for too long. It's tough to get back out of the tank, and a long drop to the floor.

The last few goons wait inside the saucer, which seals on your entry. When you take the relic from the upper chamber, Nevada is history.

NEVADA DESERT

South Pacific Islands

Coastal Village
Crash Site
Mudubu Gorge
Temple of Puna

SECRET 3 secrets?

Well, there might be three Secrets. There might also be four. The wide-open nature of the Coastal Village comes complete with two different routes toward the village itself. Two of the Secrets in the level are found no matter which path you choose, while one Secret on each path is unique. If you know when to backtrack, you can actually pick up all four. The screen actually says "4 of 3." Cool. The route we recommend is a combination of the path through the trapdoor in the hut and the Serpent Stone hunt to access the village. The walkthrough covers the easy route first, without going through the hut trapdoor. That's the obvious path, so it might be the one that you've already chosen. If not, consider finding the Smuggler's Key and entering through the hut. That way, you don't have to miss any part of the level and all four Secret areas are yours to pilfer.

1

2

Once you have the Smuggler's Key (if you're taking the hut route) and have found the first Secret, the easy route leads down behind the yellowish ledge. Be ready to backflip when the first tribesman emerges from the brush. The natives are tough, but not particularly dangerous until they start blowing poison darts.

The Coastal Village level ends at a small hut above a quicksand mire; but there are two distinct paths through the wide-open level.

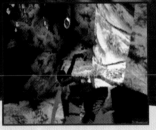

As the level begins, turn to the right and swim into the lagoon. On the floor of the area below is a square block and the Smuggler's Key.

Swim toward the main beach and pull up onto the rock with the Small Medi Pak.

SECRET

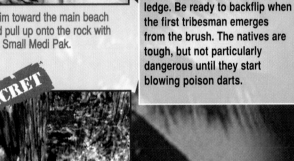

Turn your back to the coast and spy several flat rocks along the cliffs.

Run, jump, and grab the edge of the slope, then shimmy right to reach flat ground.

Jump to the square, flat section of ground, then run, jump, and grab the distant platform to claim the MP5 ammo.

One of the routes starts in the hut with the trapdoor. The Smuggler's Key opens the hole.

The more obvious route heads down behind the yellowish ridge. Once you slide down, you can't come back.

Follow the cave up into a bushy area where a tribesman hides.

Run, jump, and grab the platform in the middle of the mire. When you stand up, a dart trap activates. Stay still, then run and jump to safety.

The area with the large trees is wide open, with several slightly different routes across the falls, which include jumping in the water. Don't overlook that Save Crystal on the path below the trees.

Up above the mire, you can see the footbridge that is part of the alternative route.

Follow the cave to an opening, ready for more native resistance.

4

Collecting the three Serpent Stones is a quick task, providing you know where to look. The biggest trick is getting back out from behind the falls, since the central platform slopes away from you and it's easy to over-jump. Stand back from the edge of the exit, facing the water. Stand near the wall farthest away from the platform and jump forward. Use the walk button to stick the landing.

Just to the left as you come through the mire, climb onto the tree roots. From there, you can grab the nearby ledge and pull up.

If you're feeling ambitious, you can make a series of jumps away from the direction of the mire, along the cliff to some Shotgun shells.

Follow the branch that runs parallel to the footbridge.

SECRET

Run, jump, and grab the branch where you can see the first Serpent Stone. There are three to find.

At the opposite end of the branch where you find the first Serpent Stone, pull up to the ledge obscured by the foliage and collect the ammo.

From the branch with the first Serpent Stone, slide down to the ground.

You can see a Save Crystal through the large trees from the edge of the ledge, facing the waterfall.

Drop down and grab the crystal and continue along the path. Jump behind the falls to enter the dark chamber.

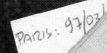

SOUTH PACIFIC

5 Once you open the main village, it's a quick trip to the end of the level. The village is the juncture where the two alternate routes through the level converge. The Serpent Stones are one means of entrance. The other is the long, white slope that you notice off to the right when you first drop down to hut level.

6 As you first come into the village, there are paths leading left and right past the huts in either direction. To the left is the mechanism which opens up the pathway on the right. When you come back through the village after spinning the wheel mechanism, there'll be a tribesman waiting on the pathway. He'll try to lead you into an ambush back near the village: a sniper will be waiting on the ledge high and to the right.

You'll find the second of the Serpent Stones behind the falls. Stand back from the edge of the ledge and jump from an angle to exit. Stick the landing.

From the platform in the center of the falls, run, jump, and grab the ladder. Climb up.

Follow the passageway and climb up the long ladder to the upper area.

Kill the tribesman on the ledge, then run, jump, and grab another ledge from there.

Jump to the outer ledge near the third Serpent Stone, then jump around the corner, mindful of the torch, and claim the prize.

Slide down from the ledge where the third stone sat, and place all three jewels in the hallway fixtures. The entrance to the main village opens.

Kill the warrior on the high ledge, then claim the Small Medi Pack. Down below, trouble comes from the left. The hut on the right holds a rocket.

As you come down the hill, follow the pathway leading beside the hut on the left. The warrior that appears is blowing poison darts.

Follow the pathway to the area near the large swamp. Kill the warrior on the ledge and turn the wheel. Expect trouble en route back to the village.

Don't even think about going for that Large Medi Pack. Pass by the hut to find another area of the village.

In the second section of the village, the goal is to open the tree house, then raise the mesh above a fiery hallway. When you pull up on the ledge below the tree house, circle around to the left and take the long hallway all the way to the end, where another dart blower appears. Better to get him out in the open and whack him quickly, than to let him lurk around.

Enter the new area with caution—after first climbing up above to take the shells. Check between the huts, where an ambush awaits.

Through the central path between the huts, look to the right. Light a Flare and watch your back when you pillage the Secret cave.

To the right of the tree house is a ledge you can climb. Check the huts upstairs. Be wary of another dart blower.

When you spin the wheel in the hut, the trapdoor below the tree house opens and a tribesman attacks.

From the tree house window, stand and jump to the roof in front of you, then jump immediately and grab to reach the ledge.

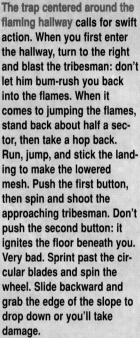

The trap centered around the flaming hallway calls for swift action. When you first enter the hallway, turn to the right and blast the tribesman: don't let him bum-rush you back into the flames. When it comes to jumping the flames, stand back about half a sector, then take a hop back. Run, jump, and stick the landing to make the lowered mesh. Push the first button, then spin and shoot the approaching tribesman. Don't push the second button: it ignites the floor beneath you. Very bad. Sprint past the circular blades and spin the wheel. Slide backward and grab the edge of the slope to drop down or you'll take damage.

Blast the bad guy lurking in the hall and follow the passage. Hop across the upper area, mindful of the hole in the floor.

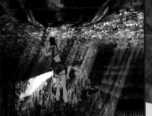

Jump from the top of the far hut and grab the vines above. Monkey-swing to the end of the line. Turn right and then stay to the left at the intersection.

The button in the hut raises a grating that allows you to get across the flames.

Sprint past the razor disks and spin the wheel to open the trapdoor in the pool. Slide backward, then hang and drop down the slope.

There's a crocodile lurking in the tunnel that you access from the hallway wheel. Perhaps you can roll at the left-hand corner and retreat back to the safety of the shore.

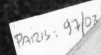

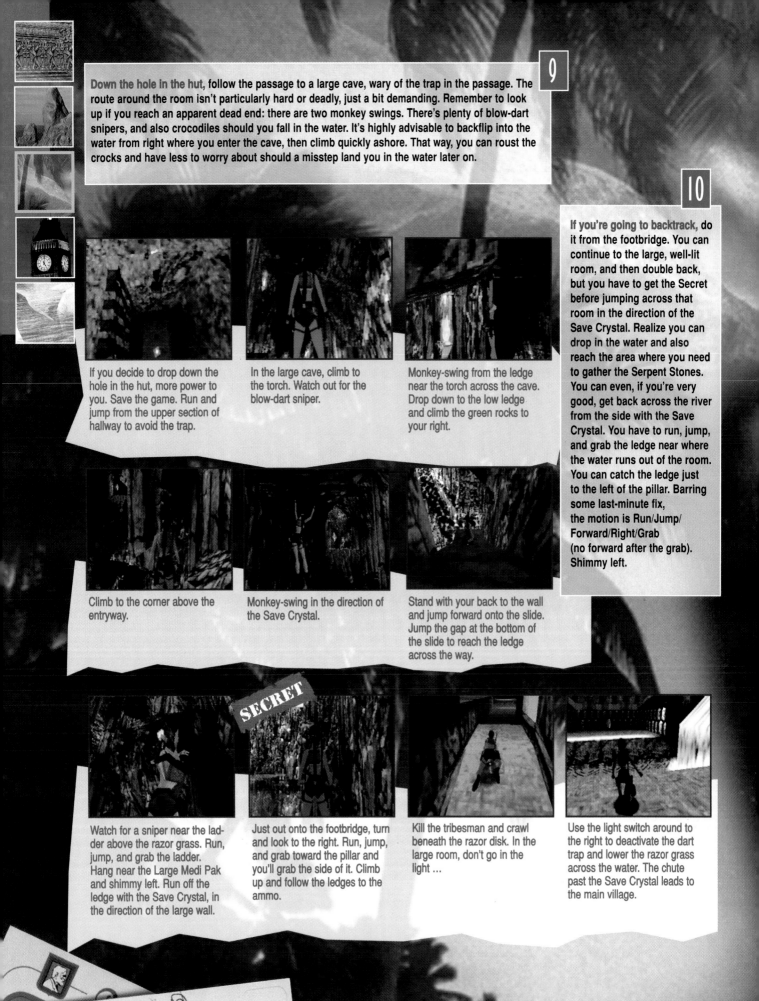

9

Down the hole in the hut, follow the passage to a large cave, wary of the trap in the passage. The route around the room isn't particularly hard or deadly, just a bit demanding. Remember to look up if you reach an apparent dead end: there are two monkey swings. There's plenty of blow-dart snipers, and also crocodiles should you fall in the water. It's highly advisable to backflip into the water from right where you enter the cave, then climb quickly ashore. That way, you can roust the crocks and have less to worry about should a misstep land you in the water later on.

10

If you're going to backtrack, do it from the footbridge. You can continue to the large, well-lit room, and then double back, but you have to get the Secret before jumping across that room in the direction of the Save Crystal. Realize you can drop in the water and also reach the area where you need to gather the Serpent Stones. You can even, if you're very good, get back across the river from the side with the Save Crystal. You have to run, jump, and grab the ledge near where the water runs out of the room. You can catch the ledge just to the left of the pillar. Barring some last-minute fix, the motion is Run/Jump/Forward/Right/Grab (no forward after the grab). Shimmy left.

If you decide to drop down the hole in the hut, more power to you. Save the game. Run and jump from the upper section of hallway to avoid the trap.

In the large cave, climb to the torch. Watch out for the blow-dart sniper.

Monkey-swing from the ledge near the torch across the cave. Drop down to the low ledge and climb the green rocks to your right.

Climb to the corner above the entryway.

Monkey-swing in the direction of the Save Crystal.

Stand with your back to the wall and jump forward onto the slide. Jump the gap at the bottom of the slide to reach the ledge across the way.

SECRET

Watch for a sniper near the ladder above the razor grass. Run, jump, and grab the ladder. Hang near the Large Medi Pak and shimmy left. Run off the ledge with the Save Crystal, in the direction of the large wall.

Just out onto the footbridge, turn and look to the right. Run, jump, and grab toward the pillar and you'll grab the side of it. Climb up and follow the ledges to the ammo.

Kill the tribesman and crawl beneath the razor disk. In the large room, don't go in the light …

Use the light switch around to the right to deactivate the dart trap and lower the razor grass across the water. The chute past the Save Crystal leads to the main village.

South Pacific Islands

Coastal Village

Crash Site

Muoubu Gorge

Temple of Puna

SECRET

3 secrets

The Crash Site is an awesome level, full of serious combat and deep puzzles. You probably want to save the game after all of the major bits, but that's one of the best things about Crash Site: it's easily compartmentalized. Of course, make sure that you pick up any Secrets in the area before doing each save: the next puzzle or battle in line may very well kill you, and it's nice not to have to do a lot of backtracking when you can avoid it. The raptors here are vile, vicious things. Use the MP5 when you can see them coming, or the Desert Eagle on those occasions when you have to fight in close quarters. When it comes to fighting the T-Rex, utilize the resident raptors. They have been known to bring the big beast down without Lara ever having to flex a trigger finger.

SECRET

Use the Swamp Map to navigate the dangerous mire. All of the jumps are the running variety. Run, jump, and grab the final distance.

Before you make the final jump from the swamp, jump off to the left and pull up into the small chamber. To jump back, run and jump from the very corner of the pad below the Secret.

Test out the MP5 on the first of many raptors, the one lurking in the fog. Climb the rocks through the fog.

Notice that the soldiers are your friends: as long as you don't shoot them, they return the favor. If you do inadvertently wing one, go ahead and finish him off, and he may give up some ammo. Use the Desert Eagle when you backflip to the tree limb. Note: In order to get to the limb from which you shoot the carcass, you have to jump and grab the edge of the slope and shimmy right. From the flat area, jump up to the small ledge in the corner. From there you can jump and grab the level with the carcass on it. There's also a Secret nearby.

In the area above, slay the raptor to the left, then take the path to the right. Look behind the large tree to find a dark hallway.

Rid the room of leapin' lizards and gather the goodies. Throw the two Switches inside to open the exit.

In the large open area, help out with the raptor trouble. Then head down the hallway to the right of the falls. In the dark, the hallway turns to the right.

Climb the ladder, then backflip and jump from the slope to the branch above. Be ready for action.

Shoot the raptor carcass and it drops to the stream below. That occupies the piranhas indefinitely.

Before you jump down into the stream, jump and grab the high branch. Be careful walking on the irregular limb.

Drop down into the stream and pull the Switch while the fish feed nearby.

SOUTH PACIFIC

The dark room with the three Switches is a nasty raptor trap, as the darkness leaves you very vulnerable. Don't burn up a bunch of Flares trying to get a good look at the crew. Throw a Switch, roll, run, and jump to the safety of the nearby box. From there, chase off the raptors in the vicinity, and make sure there are none behind you in the shadows before you hop down to throw the next Switch. You'll kill them all eventually, but you just have to get them out of the room long enough to throw another Switch. After that, the whole gang will be back to bother you again. As they retreat down the hallway in ever-increasing numbers, you may be able to bag several raptors at once with a well-placed Grenade.

You might lob a couple of Grenades into the hallway to help thin out the raptors.

The dark interior makes a prime raptor hunting ground. Use the box to get out of their reach.

Each time you pull a Switch, more raptors are released.

The T-Rex battle is quite cool, so you have some inducement for getting close to the big beast: throwing the Switches which open the exit. When you are ambushed upon arriving in the upper area, don't be so quick to shoot the raptors. They usually make quick work of the soldier unless you intervene with more than Pistols. You can run past them and down the slope. Disperse the lizards and take the Small Medi Pack. When you take the key from the nest, the torch near the first sealed door lights and the door opens. Throw the Switch inside and a distant door opens back by the water pools. If you can throw that Switch, you gain access to the upper area (through the first hall) and any raptors in the area will come down to chew on the T-Rex. While that's going on, you can go back to the upper area and get the Secret. If any raptors come back up top, it's because the T-Rex lost the fight.

Watch your back—and your health—as you pull the Switches. Roll and run to the box.

When all three Switches have been pulled, jump and grab from the box to reach the upper area. Take Lieutenant Tuckerman's Key, wary of the raptor ambush.

Double back to the pathway near the crashed plane and you should find a small, dimly lit corridor.

Follow the corridor to the ledge above the open area.

Collect the ammo. When you venture out toward the soldier, raptors attack from either side. Roll and run back to the ledge.

You can either kill the raptors or let them live. They have a tendency to attack the T-Rex living below.

If you leave the soldier alive, he helps out with the T-Rex, but he's little more than an appetizer.

The worst feature of the T-Rex area is the small pools of water. Wading through them makes Lara a proverbial sitting duck. Use the small tufts of dry ground to keep moving through the area when the T-Rex arrives, and notice that you have to take the corner wide to avoid getting hip-deep in dinosaur.

5

The large area below has two sealed doors, and the T-Rex nest.

Take Commander Bishop's Key from his body in the nest. The T-Rex appears near the water.

6

The area with the small pools is a death trap.

The T-Rex's massive jaws are capable of killing Lara with a single munch.

Sprint past the big brute toward the lit torch at the far end of the area. Throw the Switch inside and roll.

Even if you kill the T-Rex and everything else in the vicinity, you can expect a single raptor to arrive when you throw the second green-hall Switch. Of course, knowing he's on the way, use the MP5 sight on him from a safe distance. Getting to the Secret up in the tree limbs, above the upper area, can be a bit tedious. Line up Lara's head so that the peak of the tree limb frames her head as she's standing on the edge of the ledge below. Jump forward and grab: you want to have one hand on either side of the limb's peak in order for her to grab hold and pull up. You can take the Large Medi Pack relatively easily by skipping over the small gap between limbs near the tree trunk. Make sure that you jump for the Flares at the tallest gap between the limb and the tree canopy, and stick the landing.

You can peck away at the T-Rex from the safety of the short hallway, or run past him to the second Switch, which the first Switch made accessible.

Throwing the second Switch opens the exit. If you left anything alive in the upper area, they can now get down to this level.

Most of the time, any remaining raptors will go after the T-Rex.

A single raptor comes out when you pull the second Switch. Three raptors against one T-Rex is actually a pretty even fight.

With the T-Rex behind you, collect the Secret before you save the game. Jump and grab on either side of the peaked branch from the ledge below.

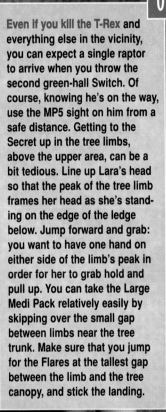

SOUTH PACIFIC

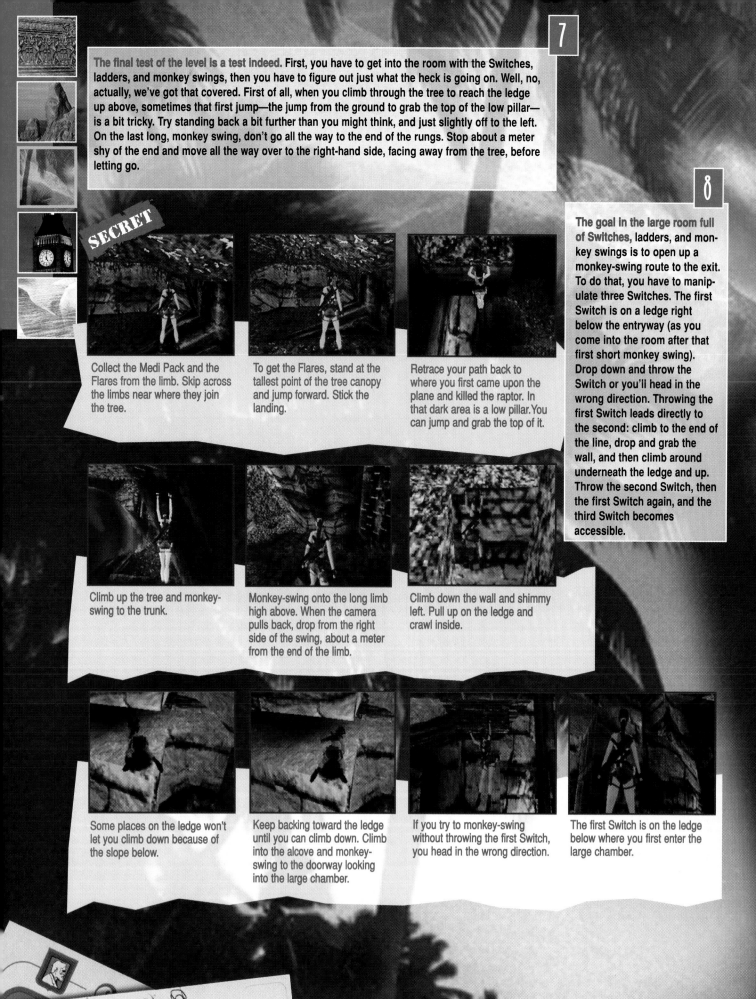

The final test of the level is a test indeed. First, you have to get into the room with the Switches, ladders, and monkey swings, then you have to figure out just what the heck is going on. Well, no, actually, we've got that covered. First of all, when you climb through the tree to reach the ledge up above, sometimes that first jump—the jump from the ground to grab the top of the low pillar—is a bit tricky. Try standing back a bit further than you might think, and just slightly off to the left. On the last long, monkey swing, don't go all the way to the end of the rungs. Stop about a meter shy of the end and move all the way over to the right-hand side, facing away from the tree, before letting go.

The goal in the large room full of Switches, ladders, and monkey swings is to open up a monkey-swing route to the exit. To do that, you have to manipulate three Switches. The first Switch is on a ledge right below the entryway (as you come into the room after that first short monkey swing). Drop down and throw the Switch or you'll head in the wrong direction. Throwing the first Switch leads directly to the second: climb to the end of the line, drop and grab the wall, and then climb around underneath the ledge and up. Throw the second Switch, then the first Switch again, and the third Switch becomes accessible.

SECRET

Collect the Medi Pack and the Flares from the limb. Skip across the limbs near where they join the tree.

To get the Flares, stand at the tallest point of the tree canopy and jump forward. Stick the landing.

Retrace your path back to where you first came upon the plane and killed the raptor. In that dark area is a low pillar. You can jump and grab the top of it.

Climb up the tree and monkey-swing to the trunk.

Monkey-swing onto the long limb high above. When the camera pulls back, drop from the right side of the swing, about a meter from the end of the limb.

Climb down the wall and shimmy left. Pull up on the ledge and crawl inside.

Some places on the ledge won't let you climb down because of the slope below.

Keep backing toward the ledge until you can climb down. Climb into the alcove and monkey-swing to the doorway looking into the large chamber.

If you try to monkey-swing without throwing the first Switch, you head in the wrong direction.

The first Switch is on the ledge below where you first enter the large chamber.

That third **Switch is a bear,** as you might imagine. Monkey-swing around and you find a dead end, even though you flipped the Switch. About-face at the dead end and climb down the wall. Climb to the very bottom, so that Lara is just hanging by her hands, and then climb back onto the ladder. Climb up just far enough so that Lara's feet are on the very bottom of the wall, slightly sticking out into space. From that position, you can backflip to the ledge where the third Switch waits. Once you throw the Switch, jump back to the ladder and climb to the ledge just above and to the right. From there, you can run and jump to a slope near the center of the large chamber. Grab the edge of the slope and shimmy to the right. Look behind you as well as you can. Try to catch a glimpse of the central pillar. As long as you can't see too much of it when you look over your left and right shoulders, you know it's right behind you. Pull up and backflip to the pillar. Return to the monkey swing and make one last trip around the room. The third Switch opens the path to the plane.

9

Once you throw the first Switch, monkey-swing to the wall nearby and climb down to the second Switch.

Jump from the second Switch ledge to the central pillar with the Save Crystal.

From the central pillar, about-face, run, jump, and grab the ledge back near the entrance.

Throw the first Switch again and take the long route on the monkey swing. Climb down the wall near the dead end. Backflip from the very bottom of the ladder to reach the alcove.

Once you make it safely back from the third Switch (See box 9), monkey-swing through to a new chamber.

10

The final battle staged with the plane's big gun is impressive, if not terribly demanding. The raptors tend to alternate right and left, so just keep sweeping the gun. Make a note to go check that smoldering soldier for ammo. Notice that you can change the elevation of the gun and protect a very small perimeter. That probably works best. When the raptors stop arriving—after a considerable amount of time—look high and to the left of the gun, and blast open two walls across the river. You reach that area—the end of the level—by jumping from the plane's wingtip.

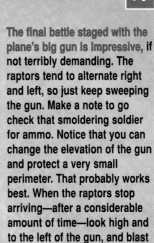

Run, jump, and grab the limb, then run and jump from there to the top of the plane.

Inside the plane, dispose of the raptor and use both keys in the cockpit.

With the power in the cockpit turned on, check the lower area of the plane.

Throw the Switch below and the big gun extends into the outdoors where a major battle is brewing.

Cut loose on the raptors and any unfortunate soldiers in the area. Across the river, in the corner of the structure on the right, are two walls that also blow open. That's the Crash Site exit.

South Pacific Islands

Coastal Village
Crash Site
Mudubu Gorge
Temple of Puna

SECRET 3 secrets

The Mudubu Gorge is an enthralling, maddening trip through whitewater and high places, and another level featuring a major shortcut. In Mudubu, you can opt to travel the walls of the gorge aways before finding a Kayak to play with, or you can go directly for the boat from the very beginning of the level. The path we outline here is a combination of the two. There's no real reason to get into the first Kayak unless you're doing the level for time. And you will miss Secrets if you get in that first boat. But, if you open up the area to the boat, you can pilfer valuable ammo, and then continue on from the same ledge where the level begins. Cool. When it comes to the Kayak, get familiar with the controls in the pool before you hit the rapids. It's important to note that Lara can paddle backward stronger than she can paddle forward. That's the key to defeating the worst of the rapids. One final note: Be wary of the little, lime green dragonettes that populate the gorge. Their breath is poisonous, so take them out in a hurry. They'll also try to shove you off of high ledges.

1

2

Check the area. In addition to the pack of bats, there's a dragon in the trees, and another living beneath the ledge of the gorge.

Climb down the pillars. Take a step back from the edge and stand and jump to the central block. From there, you can jump and grab the distant rocks and shimmy either right or left.

Shimmy right and you'll find a Switch that opens a trapdoor back near the start of the level.

Once you collect the goodies from the room above the first boat room, return to the ledge where the level began and continue on. If you get in the boat, you ride the rapids straight to the tunnel system that frames the main puzzle of the level, but you miss a lot of good stuff along the way. A good place to save is after you jump past the slope toward the opening in the low cliff face, if you haven't already.

You can get back to the start by backflipping from the slope to the block in the center of the river.

Back near the start of the level, check under the overhang, where the bats came from. Collect the ammo from up above, but return to the ledge below (See box 1).

Return to the far side of the gorge, and this time shimmy to the left. You can hang, then drop and grab the ledge below. Also, above this area is the monkey swing that takes you back across the gorge.

Follow the trail along the shore and jump past the slope to the flatland near the opening.

Past the sealed door, hang, drop, and jump from the second ledge, and you backflip over the razor grass.

When you crawl into the space, a lime green dragon comes out to breathe in your face. Not good. Standing upright before it can poison you takes nerve.

Collect the Save Crystal from the dead end, and watch for a lurking dragon on the way back.

The first Secret of the level is a real challenge. There's ammo on the floor when you pass behind the waterfall, before you monkey-swing to the platform. The slide and grab is particularly tough. Use a straight jump and a late grab to try and get some air. In order to get the Save Crystal, you have to jump over the central pillar and collect the prize on the fly, grabbing the pillar beyond for safety. A dragon appears on the floor below (didn't want you to miss a cheap kill) but don't go down there. Continue on the pathway off the ledge, and you'll reemerge on the main route.

Clean up the stairway back through the crawl space and push the button to open the sealed door.

Through the opened door, a waterfall beckons from the left.

SECRET

Behind the waterfall, collect the ammo from floor level and monkey-swing to the ledge above the slope.

First, you have to slide, then jump and grab the tall pillar. Run and jump across the central pillar to grab the Save Crystal, and continue in that direction.

Out of the Secret area, run, jump, and grab the climbable cliff face. At the top, the next Secret is to your right.

Just in case that first Secret wasn't tough enough, here's another beauty. The backflip itself is tough, since the slope you're trying to hit is steep and Lara tends to over-shoot it. Rather than trying to tell you an exact position, we suggest you start as far away as possible and backflip to get an idea of how much distance you have to travel. Work your way back until you clear the ledge and hit the slope. There's not much margin for error. Grab the bottom of the slope and shim-my right, then drop down to the small thatch platform. It's a simple task to pilfer the shack, but getting back on the beaten path is merci-less. We highly recommend that you save the game before trying the return leap, please. It's a stan-dard running jump to the distant, low ledge, but you have to jump so that you don't bang your head. Lean back toward the ledge as you fall. It's possible to do this without grabbing, but we've had more suc-cess flattening out that trajectory with the grab—once we're past the point of the obstruction. You should land with your feet on the ledge.

Backflip from the ledge above to the steep slope, and grab the edge when you slide down. Shimmy right and drop to the short platform below.

To make it back from the shack, you have to run and jump from the short platform, mindful of your head, to the ledge across the way (See box 3).

Back on the trail, past the ledge where you backflip to the Secret, clear out the crocodiles near the Kayak. The Switch that opens the gate is below the corner, beneath the dark water.

When you come through the gate from the pool, row back-ward furiously to slow your descent, and then move into the cove to the right.

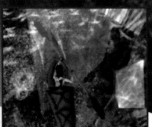

Fight the current around the perimeter of the lagoon and into the niche with the Save Crystal. This is a decent place to save the game.

SOUTH PACIFIC

There's no real substitute for practical experience when it comes to the Kayak, but paddling backward to fight the current is a big key. Over the first big falls, however, you just want to hug the right-hand wall and go with the flow. If you try to slow yourself down, the current pulls you to the center of the river, and thus toward the rock below. The current pulls you around to face the blade trap easily enough, just start paddling backward to reach the trip line that shuts off the trap. Over the second falls—after you disable the blade trap—fight the current until you're almost at a standstill. Even if you bonk the rock below, it's usually not very painful. And slowing your momentum is crucial to fighting the left turn into the rapids.

Down through the trip lines, you find that as you get more familiar with the Kayak, rowing backward to avoid the trip lines is relatively easy stuff, just anticipate each turn, and get the boat sideways so that you can row off to one side, away from the rope triggers. When you make the last evasive maneuver, you have to row backward just far enough to make it around the safe turn, but not so far that you go all the way to the wall and get caught in the current. If you go down that other path, you're in for a merciless beating, or a quick game reload. There is a Save Crystal in the waterway that you can use to save the game if you're clinging to life. If you're having a really hard time getting through the narrow gap that pushes you in the proper direction, consider simply tripping the last of the traps and heading on through the razor grass. Yeah, it stings a little, but it probably won't kill you. Not like that other route.

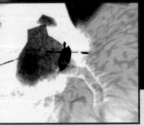

Over the first falls, stick to the wall on the right to avoid the big boulder, as well as the trip line.

Around the bend, the current pulls you to the right. Row backward to the trip line that deactivates the blades.

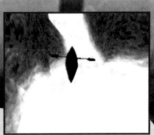

Over the second falls, the rock is on the left. Row backward to arrest your momentum at the bottom of the falls.

Row backward like a madwoman to keep from getting sucked over the rapids. Don't try to change direction, as you can't afford to bounce into the rock walls upstream.

In the dark cavern, follow the stream around to the right.

Negotiate the run by rowing backward to slow yourself and picking your way around the trip lines.

At the last trip line, turn to one side and row backward, but not too far: just make it around the corner.

Just past the last trip line, begin rowing forward to make it into the narrow opening. This is the toughest part of the run, but it beats the heck out of going the other direction.

The last stretch of the rapids is marked with pockets of razor grass. Keep left initially; then go with the flow.

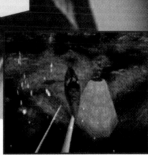

Finally, you're dumped into a larger chamber.

7

In order to pull the plug, you have to negotiate the series of monkey swings, and then realize that the apparent dead end is just one little leap of faith. The area with the bright waterfall is interesting because you can get the Secret credit by jumping across the falls, but you must take the Kayak into the small cave in order to get the Save Crystal. Getting up the tunnel is a bit tricky because hitting a wall slows you enough that the current pushes you backward. Keep to the center and make only minor course adjustments. If you get desperate, try rowing backward up the tunnel.

Removing the huge plug from the bottom of the pool is the main puzzle of the level.

Off the plug room, to the left of a whitewater tunnel, is a relatively quiet avenue you should explore.

8

SECRET

As long as you can keep from banging the walls, you can make it into a large chamber with a bright waterfall.

Behind the bright waterfall, paddle back and get the Save Crystal. There are other goodies on the shore that you'll have to get later.

Back in the plug room, take the greenish tunnel.

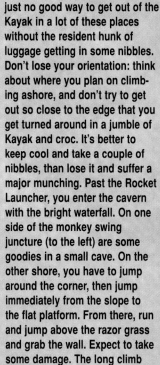

The whole crocodile thing is kind of depressing. There's just no good way to get out of the Kayak in a lot of these places without the resident hunk of luggage getting in some nibbles. Don't lose your orientation: think about where you plan on climbing ashore, and don't try to get out so close to the edge that you get turned around in a jumble of Kayak and croc. It's better to keep cool and take a couple of nibbles, than lose it and suffer a major munching. Past the Rocket Launcher, you enter the cavern with the bright waterfall. On one side of the monkey swing juncture (to the left) are some goodies in a small cave. On the other shore, you have to jump around the corner, then jump immediately from the slope to the flat platform. From there, run and jump above the razor grass and grab the wall. Expect to take some damage. The long climb up the wall is uneventful.

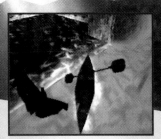

Up the greenish tunnel, a crocodile awaits your frantic exit from the Kayak.

Once you settle the score with the croc, monkey-swing out over the chamber, and time your swings to pass safely by the flaming faces.

Jump to the distant ledge, and claim the **Rocket Launcher**. Continue up the rock near the weapon.

Follow the trail to the chamber with the bright waterfall. You can run, jump, and grab to get the ammo across the falls. If you didn't get the Save Crystal for some reason, you'll get the Secret sound when you jump.

Double back down the shore from the bright waterfall and climb to the ledge on the left.

SOUTH PACIFIC

Up the long wall climb, you find a hallway where boulders roll down, and Lara must crouch beneath low ledges to let each boulder pass overhead. When you come into the short room with the central walkway, you can walk out pretty far before the boulder drops behind you. Walk out a couple of sectors, then turn and back over the edge of the walkway, grabbing to shimmy over the flames. Pull up at the far end and the boulder should stay put. In the flaming hallway, stand half a sector back from the flames and jump over. Don't grab. The boulder above releases very quickly, and if you grab you stumble and are unceremoniously mowed down.

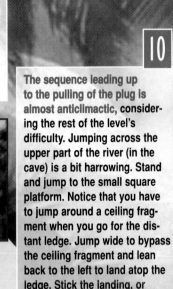

The sequence leading up to the pulling of the plug is almost anticlimactic, considering the rest of the level's difficulty. Jumping across the upper part of the river (in the cave) is a bit harrowing. Stand and jump to the small square platform. Notice that you have to jump around a ceiling fragment when you go for the distant ledge. Jump wide to bypass the ceiling fragment and lean back to the left to land atop the ledge. Stick the landing, or you'll likely slip right over the side of the ledge and into the water. When you ride the big funnel down, realize that you need full health and a little luck. We've made it down entirely unscathed, and we've also hit bottom like a wet sack of rocks. Try to ride on the edge of the funnel, and follow it around, instead of paddling straight into the hole. Down below, the same Switch that opens the exit also releases a pair of crocs into the water. Because the Switch is underneath a low underwater ledge, this can be very bad. Roll as soon as you pull the Switch and get out of the water in a big hurry.

Monkey-swing out to the juncture. After you hear the bats chatter, stop moving forward. Pivot left and drop off at the wall.

Collect the ammo from the left-hand shore and monkey-swing over to the opposite side of the stream. Jump around the corner to the slope, and from there to the platform. Jump back and grab the wall. Climb.

When you reach the outside area, look for a tunnel on your right. Inside the tunnel, you have to duck a number of rolling boulders (See box 8).

Past the boulders, you arrive upstream. Run and jump to the platform on the right and climb to the crawl space.

Through the crawl space, stand and jump to the central platform, and then run and jump to the ledge beyond. Watch your head and stick the landings.

Ride the rope slider down. You have to jump off on the entryway ledge, or you'll take a small amount of damage from landing in the room.

Climb the tall texture, ready for a dragon ambush from the right, at the top.

Throw the Switch in the outer hall to pull the plug. When the torch lights in the nearby hallway, another dragon comes out to play.

Return to the Kayak and head down the drain. You have to ride the edge or you'll take serious damage from the fall into the chamber below.

Kill the crocodile. Beneath the ledge is a Switch that opens the exit and release a pair of crocs into the small pool.

South Pacific Islands

- COASTAL VILLAGE
- CRASH SITE
- MUDUBU GORGE
- TEMPLE OF PUNA

SECRET
secret

The South Pacific Temple of Puna level is a quick trip once you know how to defeat the main puzzle—a room covered with huge blades, with four buttons on the walls that you must reach without being cruelly cut down. Right from the beginning the residents object to your arrival. You almost invariably get poisoned, so follow the stairs to the crawl space and rid that area of enemies before returning to explore the area. You should really only save the game once in the temple, right before you begin the final boulder puzzle. You need to get past the first puzzle, but that's near the beginning of the level. Once you're past the boulder trap, there's no reason to save before fighting Puna. The boulder trap is quick and relatively easy, and you need not fear the boss.

The temple begins in a hostile intersection. Draw your weapon and look to the right.

Blast the tribesmen in the hallway. If you get poisoned, quickly clean the stairs of all the enemies before having a Medi Pack.

In the lower area, the gate is the entrance to the boss's lair.

The big puzzle could kill you several times before you even know what to do. **The whole trick is to stand in the corner at an angle, not with your back flat to the wall. You can stand flat to the wall like that and not take damage, but the margin for error is much greater. Things are hard enough already.**

The large room with the boulder on the ramp is the final stage of the trap leading up to the boss.

The enemies attack as soon as this level gets underway.

Follow the stairway up, ready for one last blow-dart warrior on the long switchback staircase.

At the top of the stairs, crawl through to the level's big puzzle.

The line of rolling blades rakes the room from end to end. Very bad.

Jump from the upper ledge (sliding slows you down) and sprint to the near right corner as the blades roll away.

Quickly orient yourself so that Lara is in the very corner of the room, standing at an angle with the corner directly behind her.

SOUTH PACIFIC

3

Don't even worry about getting the Save Crystal until you throw all four Switches and open the exit. There's no reason to go saving the game until this is over, even then you should hold off awhile. The corners of the large chamber seem to be a little sticky, though perhaps it's just orienting yourself at an angle and pressing there so desperately that makes things difficult. Consider jumping out of the corner, or backflipping out. The backflip is quick, and lets you line up nicely with the button nearby: you're not going to have time to sidestep into position.

4

Jump the gap between two of the blades to reach the far end of the room. Hit the ground and start sprinting for the far end of the room and you should have just enough time to get face first into a corner.

When the blade rolls back toward the far end of the room, you have a few seconds to get out of the corner and hit the Switch.

It takes skill and nerves of steel to get back to the safe position before the blades make their quick return.

When the blades head to the far end of the room, sprint across to the corner near the Switch.

You can go face-first into the corner and still be safe, as long as you're standing correctly.

Don't turn to face the center of the room until the blades reverse away again. If you're turning in the corner space, the blade makes contact.

To get to the other end of the room, you'll have to step out as the blades roll away, and line up with one of the "axles."

Jump the gap between a set of blades and sprint for a distant corner.

Keep your nerve and watch your health. As long as you're relatively healthy, you can survive a couple of nicks.

It can be a little sticky to get out of the corners. Don't hesitate to return to a corner if you don't get out cleanly.

Consider backflipping out of the corners. A small turn sets you up nicely with the nearby button.

When the fourth button is pushed, the distant door opens. Don't forget that Save Crystal, but don't feel like you have to get it on the way to the door.

From the safety of the door, you can see that the Save Crystal is slightly off-center in the room. Let the blades roll to the left.

5

Once you solve the blades puzzle, the temptation is to save the game right away. Don't do it. The next puzzle has a box you can pull out—and there's nothing else that can kill you between there and the boulder puzzle. Save before you start the boulders rolling.

6

You can actually solve the spiked ceiling puzzle by frantically pulling all three Switches, the last being the one right near the exit. It's very close, and entirely unnecessary. Pull out the box as soon as you hit the ground, and the spikes are stopped. Throw the Switches and the door opens.

Sprint out for the prize, ready to roll just as you reach it.

Sprint back for safety. As long as you keep a reasonably straight line—and aim for the left-hand side of the open door, you can make it.

Down the slope, the puzzle seems to require that you throw all three Switches before the ceiling tenderizes our heroine.

Although you can solve the puzzle by throwing Switches, simply pull out the box.

The spikes descend, and get stuck at the box top.

Throw all three Switches to open the door. Hang and drop down the hole.

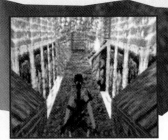

In the large room, the first of two boulders is poised for its downhill run.

When you throw the Switch, the area lights up, and the entry door seals.

SOUTH PACIFIC

7

The rolling boulders is one of those puzzles complicated by the perspective. And if you try to tap the camera back to a Lara's-eye view, all you get is a really good view of Lara getting flattened. Bank to the right out the doorway and don't start sprinting too soon. You can run in front of the first boulder until you hear it release, and then start the sprint. It becomes critical to still be able to sprint when you get out into the hallway, in front of that second rock.

8

The entry to the Temple of Puna Secret area is one of those nasty little hide-in-the-shadows types. Look above the small landing where the staircase switches back, before you head up to the crawl space. Inside is a ton of ammo for the Desert Eagle.

Sprint down the run as the big rock releases.

Sprint out the door, back into the area you saw when the level began. Make a right turn.

In the passageway, make for the Save Crystal. The flooring panels will collapse unless you stick to the center of the run, so keep moving.

As long as you don't start sprinting too soon, you should have just enough juice to make it to safety, between the two slopes.

Don't sweat it if you miss the Save Crystal on the first pass.

You can crawl back and take the Save Crystal from beneath the rock.

As you walk into the hallway, a tribesman appears on the right, near the boss's gate.

Two more enemies appear moments later on the left. Perhaps they know a Secret?

Climb back up the long staircase. At the point where it switches back, a portal opens high above. You can barely see it in the dark.

Jump from the stairs to the wall and shimmy left to the opening.

9

The boss is tough, but he's a one-trick pony. If he hits you with a lightning bolt, you're dead. However, as long as you never stand still, he can't hit you. Because he sits in his chair, he is an easy target.

In the dimly lit room, collect the precious ammo. That'll makes the next adventure a little easier.

Once you slide down the slope behind the open gate, you enter the lair.

10

If you get poisoned while fighting the boss, **don't be too quick to use a Medi Pack.** There's another of those small dragons waiting in the wings, and it'll probably poison you, as well. Don't let those little buggers bull rush you over the edge. Try to kill them with the boss in front of you, as you want to start jumping from side to side again very quickly. The half-second pause between the time when the second dragon goes up in flames and the boss renews his attack is the best time for a Small Medi Pack.

The boss sits with his back to you on a high throne. You have to approach to get his attention.

Jump from side to side, and keep those guns blazing.

A couple of times during the fight, the boss fires an odd colored bolt off to one side and summons some help.

Take care of the hired help before turning back to the boss. The boss won't attack you until the summoned enemy is dearly departed.

Don't worry too much about getting poisoned. If Puna tags you with a lightning bolt, no amount of health will save you anyway.

Keep hopping from side to side so that the lightning bolts consistently go wide.

Finally, the boss succumbs.

Collect the Small Medi Packs from the main platform. After you claim the relic, the South Pacific Islands are behind you.

SOUTH PACIFIC

South Pacific Islands

London

THAMES WHARF

ALDWYCH

LUD'S GATE

CITY

SECRET 5 secrets

Thames Wharf is one of those wonderful little levels that you could wander aimlessly for hours. It has some ambience. As you begin, your task is to obtain the Flue Room Key, and use that to access an underground playground. There's a ton of Save Crystals hereabouts, and you can move pretty easily through each area as long as you proceed with caution and nail the jumps. What that means, in practical terms, is that you should have a healthy stock of Save Crystals at the level's end. The first Secret of the wharf is nearby as the level gets underway: use the stretch of walkway leading up to the sloped wall to jump over it. Step back one step, then hop back, then run and jump. On the trip back from the Secret, you have to actually jump and grab the edge of the slope that you stand beside when you first see the crane. From there, climb the tall box to the top of the wall, and jump and grab the edge of the slope above the walkway where the level began. Just grab and then shimmy to the left before you pull up: there's a gap over there you don't want to slide into.

As the level begins, check the surrounding area and notice the sloping wall to the right. Over the wall lies your first Secret.

Run and jump over the wall using the walkway leading straight to it. Collect the Save Crystal and ammo, and utilize the tall box to climb the wall.

Across the wall, hop down to the lower platform and run and jump to the crane. Drop down to the counterweight and jump over to the ladder.

To get down to the Switch below the starting walkway, drop down to the ledge when you get the wide-angle view, then step backward off that ledge and land on a slope below. Jump almost immediately and grab the ledge with the Switch. The Switch raises the trapdoor across the way, which lets you access the room with the Flue Room Key.

SECRET

Follow the pathway down to the sloped roof. You have to jump to the central opening to avoid the barbwire.

Walk through the barbwire and rid the room of rats and other more desirable things.

Pull up out of the barbwire and return to the crane's arm above the counterweight. The route back is semi-obvious, but be careful to shimmy left before you slide back to the level start (See box 2).

Hang from the end of the walkway near the level start and you can see the ramp and the Switch below.

Step backward and drop onto the slope, then jump and grab the ledge with the Switch. Throw it and look across the gap. Run, jump, and grab to the platform with the Small Medi Pack.

Slide and drop down to the green trapdoor that was raised when you threw the Switch moments ago.

In the large, dark room, the second section of the platform on the left will collapse under Lara's weight: roll onto it and run to the adjoining section, which is solid.

To get to the Flue Room Key, you have to run and jump from the stable section of the platform high on the wall—on your immediate left when you first see the room. Run, jump, and grab: you'll hit your head on the beam above, but still manage to grab the ledge. The hallway with the aforementioned bad guy is off to the right. To lower the trapdoor that allows you to jump and grab the walkway back near the entrance to the large room, you have to drop a ledge below the large platform. Of course, you'll want to make your way to a low ledge and drop to the floor first: there's Flares, a Save Crystal, and Harpoons. A button below lets you climb back to the large platform. When you jump and grab at the crack, don't try and grab too far away: there's a ledge to catch you down below in case you blow it, but only if you're within a sector of the large platform.

Run, jump, and grab from the stable section of the platform to the distant ledge. You'll bonk your head, but you can still make the grab. Follow the hallway and take the Flue Room Key from the bad guy.

Backtrack to the ledge. To get out of the room, you need to hang from the corner of the platform, then drop and grab the platform below. That button opens the exit, which you reach by shimmying to the right along the crack (See box 3).

Back near the green trapdoor outside, you can throw the Switch on the wall to the right, then hang and drop to the level below.

Expect crow trouble when you discover the ledge above the green door: he's guarding a Secret.

SECRET

Shimmy right using the invisible ledge. There are two crawl spaces to pilfer. You'll get the Secret chime when you enter the second one.

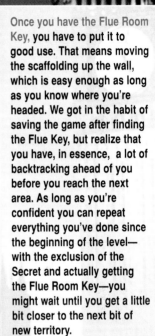

Once you have the Flue Room Key, you have to put it to good use. That means moving the scaffolding up the wall, which is easy enough as long as you know where you're headed. We got in the habit of saving the game after finding the Flue Key, but realize that you have, in essence, a lot of backtracking ahead of you before you reach the next area. As long as you're confident you can repeat everything you've done since the beginning of the level—with the exclusion of the Secret and actually getting the Flue Room Key—you might wait until you get a little bit closer to the next bit of new territory.

Return to the ledge with the green door and pull up into the dark crawl space. Follow the path to the right.

Push the button, and then double back through the crawl space. The button you see in the cinematic moves the scaffold.

From the end of the walkway with the green door, hang and drop to the slope and down to ground level. Dispose of the sniper, and don't overlook the Flares near the Save Crystal.

Utilize the stack of boxes near the ammo to climb back to the upper ledges.

Climb the ladders back up to where the level began.

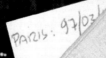

LONDON

Once the scaffold has been raised, **you can enter the Flue Room.** As long as you don't plan on waltzing out into the Flue Room inferno once you push the button, you don't need to save right there. The stretch of the level between the Flue Room and the next large puzzle is long, but not really hazardous.

Jump back over to the ledge above the green trapdoor. You don't need to throw the Switch first, but it couldn't hurt.

Utilize the long crack to shimmy the length of the building to the right.

Follow the pathway. When you come to the upper and lower passage juncture, choose the low road.

The Secret up above the burner which the Flue Room button extinguishes is a hazard, but check the pictures carefully, and remember to jump back to the hallway above the extinguished burner before dropping down into the burner hole.

You can see the scaffold far below. The button that raises it (the one that was behind the glass) is to the right.

The scaffold repositions in front of the Flue Room door.

Run and jump to the scaffold, grabbing to lower your trajectory and avoid the awning.

Smoke the crow and enter the Flue Room.

When you push the button beyond the Save Crystal, puffs of flame cross the room. Be careful on your way out: pause and wait for the flame to fade, and run through to the safe zone between the puffs.

Hang and drop from the edge of the scaffold to return to the pathway. Double back to the high road at the juncture.

Before you drop down into the hole that the Flue Room button made accessible, jump and grab the ledge, and pull up near the ammo.

Once you have the Secret, you can follow the hallways down to the underground. Wait to save the game until you start to mess with the water tanks puzzle. Check out the two nearby tanks before you throw the water-level Switch and you'll have a better idea of what's going on. Also, keep those guns at the ready as you prowl the halls near the tanks. There's guards on the prowl, sometimes near the tank and always when you go back to the water control room to manipulate the level in each tank.

SECRET

Look off to the left from where you picked up the ammo. Step onto the slope, slide, and drop to the small ledge below.

Drop down from the ledge above and collect the rocket before climbing back to the hole in the path. Jump to the path, then hang and drop through the hole from there.

Follow the passageway, jumping and grabbing from the ledge to reach the hallway with the Save Crystal.

Follow the somewhat sloping hallway, careful not to slide down without that Large Medi Pack.

Drop down into the room and dispose of the guard. This is the water control room. The Switch and the two buttons under glass help solve a big puzzle.

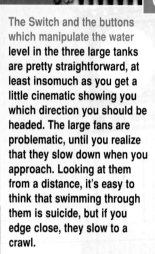

The Switch and the buttons which manipulate the water level in the three large tanks are pretty straightforward, at least insomuch as you get a little cinematic showing you which direction you should be headed. The large fans are problematic, until you realize that they slow down when you approach. Looking at them from a distance, it's easy to think that swimming through them is suicide, but if you edge close, they slow to a crawl.

When you first arrive, one of the tanks down the hallway is full of water.

The other tank is dry, and you can see a red-lit hallway off to the left, out of reach.

Throw the Switch in the water control room, and then swim down into the previously dry tank. Collect the stash and pull the Switch. A door in the floor of the other tank opens.

Throw the Switch in the water control room again and the water level lowers in the tank with the open trapdoor. Approach the blades and they slow enough for you to swim past.

Follow the passage past the underwater fans. Look for a crawl space when it dead-ends. Drop from the upper hallway to the passage below.

PARIS: 97/03

Visas

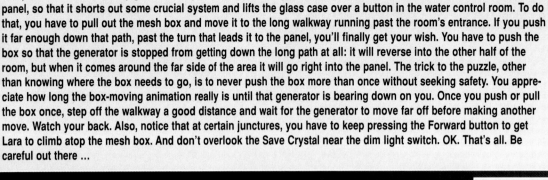

The problem of the runaway generator is particularly vexing: **you need to direct it to the small niche with the control panel, so that it shorts out some crucial system and lifts the glass case over a button in the water control room. To do that, you have to pull out the mesh box and move it to the long walkway running past the room's entrance. If you push it far enough down that path, past the turn that leads it to the panel, you'll finally get your wish. You have to push the box so that the generator is stopped from getting down the long path at all: it will reverse into the other half of the room, but when it comes around the far side of the area it will go right into the panel. The trick to the puzzle, other than knowing where the box needs to go, is to never push the box more than once without seeking safety. You appreciate how long the box-moving animation really is until that generator is bearing down on you. Once you push or pull the box once, step off the walkway a good distance and wait for the generator to move far off before making another move. Watch your back. Also, notice that at certain junctures, you have to keep pressing the Forward button to get Lara to climb atop the mesh box. And don't overlook the Save Crystal near the dim light switch. OK. That's all. Be careful out there ...**

In the dark room with the runaway generator, pull out the mesh box and push it so that the generator smashes the wall panel (See box 9).

Climb the ladder back to the water control room. You should be able to swim to the red-tinged hallway once the button is pressed. If not, flip the Switch on the wall.

Through the red-tinged hallway, swim over and relieve the guard, then press the button to make the second glass-covered Switch accessible. The large tank is dry when you go to backtrack, but there's a monkey swing above.

The last bit of the level, **leading up to the cathedral dome, is nerve-racking but not particularly dangerous. Just pretend that none of the ledges have barbwire on them and that you feel like walking for a change. No problem. Inside the dome, the central box can only be moved in one direction, and only a short distance. Climb atop it and you'll find you can climb to a flat section up above. From there, run and jump along the wall to clear the slope across the path. It's a tough jump, designed so that you might not think it's possible after trying it a couple of times. Stick very close to that wall on the left, and don't grab: you need the height to get over the slope. The Cathedral Key, alas, is a key without a home, though it does have a level all it's own. The key is a big clue that, if you have collected every last Secret in the game, you get to play a Secret Level at the end.**

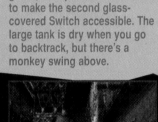

When the second button in the water control room is pressed, return to the tank that you monkey-swung above. Swim down through the opening and follow the underwater tunnel once you collect the Harpoons.

When you reach the open area, collect the underwater goodies and exit the pool into the hallway. Expect trouble.

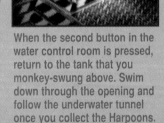

Follow the pathway through the barbwire, jumping to the crane platform and from there to the wall. Take your time: a misstep is fatal.

There's major sniper trouble lurking in the cathedral dome, as well as the last two Secrets of the level. Don't jump to the walkway on the opposite side of the dome until you get the goods.

SECRET

Push the movable block the short distance you can move it, and climb to the surface above. From near where you find the Small Medi Pack, run and jump along the wall, over the distant slope, and claim the Cathedral Key.

Before you take the exit path, look to the left, and you'll see an odd break in the fence line. Climb down the ladder and follow the path downward.

SECRET

Take the Large Medi Pack and double back to the level exit path leading away from the dome.

London

THAMES WHARF

ALDWYCH

LUD'S GATE

CITY

SECRET

5 secrets

Ask not for whom the train rolls, it rolls for thee. Aldwych is a maze of twisting hallways and dangerous tunnels, and if you don't get started in the right direction you can have a merciless time back-tracking. It's also one of those levels where you pick up a ton of items, and then carry them around for awhile thinking you must have missed something. An Old Penny? A Masonic Mallet? Hello? Keep those guns out when on patrol, as rats both large and small are in abundance. From the start of the level, lean forward and grab as you fall, and collect the Shotgun Shells before dropping into the water.

Blow open the grating in the long hallway, and climb to the upper chamber. Watch your back as you gather goodies.

Circle around and pull the box with the climbable surface.

Drop down into the ticket booth area and defend yourself. Look for another opening above a ticket booth.

The red room is a room you'll see quite enough of because you'll be backtracking through it on a regular basis. Do save the game up above the slope leading down into the drill room, once you monkey-swing through the red room. If you want to get the Secret from down below, you need to do everything just right and very quickly, as the drill comes crunching down from above.

Since you moved the box up above, you can jump up above the ticket booth and climb to a small room. Take the Maintenance Room Key and exit via the door.

Follow the right-hand escalator and run and jump the pit. Plug the immortal and check the door.

Try your key in the door and push the button in the small room to turn on the lights.

Look on the same side of the tracks as the maintenance room. With the lights on, you should find an Old Penny.

Drop down onto the deep set of tracks—the ones you must jump to reach the previous area. Sprint and duck off to the right to avoid the oncoming train.

Clean up in the red room and climb the ladder. Backflip from the top to reach the nearby ledge.

Monkey-swing along the ceiling. Be sure to make that right turn, and drop down at the wall.

LONDON

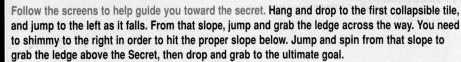

Follow the screens to help guide you toward the secret. **Hang and drop to the first collapsible tile, and jump to the left as it falls. From that slope, jump and grab the ledge across the way. You need to shimmy to the right in order to hit the proper slope below. Jump and spin from that slope to grab the ledge above the Secret, then drop and grab to the ultimate goal.**

4

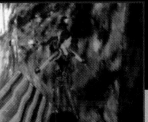

Hang and drop into the drill room, jumping immediately to the left from the collapsible platform. Slide, jump, and grab.

Quickly shimmy to the right as the blade descends. Drop from the right half of the ledge.

Drop down, and grab the edge of the slope. Pull up and back-flip, spinning in midair to grab the ledge.

Don't make the furnace traps harder than they are: **you can sidestep along the edge of the ledge and avoid getting burned. Don't overlook the button before you get to the high trap. If the trap is inactive, you passed the button just below. The button opens a trapdoor up above the red room. Don't overlook the stash in the darkened corner of the upper room before you drop through the grating.** (Although it's no problem if you miss it the first time through: You'll be back.)

SECRET

Hang and drop to the lower ledge. Now that's a Secret.

In the upper chamber, climb to the dangerous ledges and side-step right. Wait for the flames to die off, and hurry atop the block.

Climb upward. A Switch along the way activates another near-by trap and opens a trapdoor back in the red room.

Climb to the chamber above the train platform. Pop the rats and collect the prizes. Drop down to the platform.

Backtrack to the red room via the low set of tracks. Climb to the open trapdoor as you did before.

In the upper room, drop the bad guy and check the area. Drop down and pull the box to access a hallway.

Follow the passage to a greenish cooridor.

The timed button puzzle is the final step to collecting both of Solomon's Keys, which open the locks in the velvety red Mason's room. Run to the middle door, then to the most distant one, and finally to the closest. There are small ancillary hallways that let you backtrack to the pair of buttons, should you take the rooms out of order.

The Switches on the wall control the timed doors in the upper chamber. You only need to press one at a time.

The object is to raise the piece of ceiling which prevents you from swinging over to the platform in the room on the left.

Pressing the left-hand button allows you to sprint to the middle and far right rooms (See box 5).

When you backtrack through the red room, monkey-swing to the drill room. There's a second Solomon's Key in the hall up from the drill.

On your way past the ticket booths, use the Old Penny at the dark window. A Ticket appears at your feet.

When you investigate down the second escalator, you need to be quick as you run down the tracks toward the lights in the distance. A guard comes from a door on the left and attempts to duck back through another open portal. If he makes it, Lara is left in the path of the oncoming train. Push the button in the small room to enter the button puzzle area, and also open a small alcove off the tracks with a Save Crystal. Save the game before you start the button puzzle, just in case. Just inside the hallway, turn to the right and press that button. Return to the long hallway, and follow it straight and around a left-hand turn. At the very end of that long section, press the button. In the room that opens, press the button on the left. Return to the left-hand turn in the long hall: there's a button on the wall on the right, just past the turn. Press it. Return to the very first button. Press that one. Now double back to the very end of the long hall and press the button at the end one more time. The way should be open to the Mason's room, as well as a couple of tangential hidey-holes. No charge.

SECRET

Check down the second escalator. Uh oh … somebody's carrying a torch for Lara.

Blast open the grating near the mudslide and drop inside to gather the stash.

Run down the tracks to the right and shoot the guard quickly when he appears near the doors. If he makes it inside, Lara gets trained.

The button puzzle is maddening. There are four Switches in the area (See box 6).

In the room with two Switches, the right-hand one can be left alone entirely.

PARIS: 97/03

LONDON

In the Mason's room, **check near the Save Crystal for the Uzis, and watch out for those collapsible tiles. You need to run across one to get the Ornate Star from behind the curtain, so jump forward from the edge of the area behind the curtain to make it safely back to the room. Solomon's Keys let you lay hands on the Masonic Mallet. Cool.**

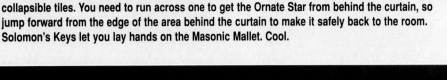

Finally, **you get to use up some of that inventory. In the case of the Ornate Star and the Masonic Mallet, stand in front of the door, not off to the right, as you might assume. You did remember to change in that Old Penny for a Ticket, didn't you?**

Once you solve the button puzzle, you can enter the Mason's room.

Notice that one of the curtains extends to the ground above a collapsible floor section. Run through the curtain and take the Ornate Star.

Put both of Solomon's Keys in the Mason's room locks, and be ready for dog trouble when you take the Masonic Mallet.

Through the other door that opens in the Mason's room, swim to the chamber. Run and jump to grab the crack in the wall and shimmy right.

SECRET

Jump to the ceiling panel and drop to the crawl space. Use the Ticket at the barrier, wary of rats and other vermin.

Use the Ornate Star in front of the door past the row of barriers. Be ready to jump back and open fire. Follow the upper hallway and backtrack.

Head down the escalator and follow the path.

Use the Masonic Mallet to open the locked door.

Follow the hallway, ready for an ambush from the right. That's a backtrack route in a few moments, but not yet.

Near the train, snuff the bad guy and check the dark end of the cavern for even more good stuff.

9

The area around the train is a little loopy, since it's hard to tell exactly what's going on as you enter the train and use that button. Just follow the obvious passages and you'll be led toward the end of the level. The backtrack to the last Secret is almost reason enough to shoot the frightened foe on sight, but you have to let him live long enough to open the small chamber with the two buttons.

Backtrack to the crack in the floor and climb into the train. Press the button and exit with a new area accessible.

Keep your finger off the trigger as you enter the dark hallway. You have to let the bad guy up ahead live, at least temporarily.

10

Follow the torch-bearer down the hallway.

Be ready for an attack as you round the final corner: two bad guys rush at you.

In the small room, press both Switches.

To backtrack to the red room, use the overpass where the bad guy jumped you just moments ago. That door was locked until he came through, and leads back to the train platform above the low tracks. Be mindful that you don't inadvertently slip down one of the ramps near the button room, as those are both level exits. Yes, they both lead to the same place. In the final Secret room, watch out for the villain lurking at the hall's intersection, off to the left.

You need to backtrack through the train, all the way to the red room. Yes, the red room.

In the hallway where you gave chase, and also near the small room with the buttons, are two ramps. Those end the level.

Use the overpass to head back to the low section of tracks.

SECRET

Up through the trapdoor in the red room, you'll see that door has opened.

Here are plenty of prizes, and even an extra kill.

PARIS: 97/03/

LONDON

London

SECRET
6 secrets

Having spoken with Bob between levels, Lara is now on friendlier terms with the monstrous results of Sophia's science. As long as you don't shoot any of the shadowy figures, you can conserve some ammo. Military men, of course, are a different matter. There are quite a few here that are heavily armed. Also, you may notice that there's a small shortcut in the level that lets you bypass the room with the giant sphinx, and forget all about the Embalming Fluid that Bob needs. That wouldn't be very sporting, of course. Also, make sure you get all the Secrets on your first pass. You can backtrack through much of the level if you're creative about it, but Lud's Gate is too big to wander if you can possibly avoid it.

Now that you've made friends, you can let the immortals be, and they'll keep to themselves.

From the room with two small pools, choose the left-hand path. Slide to the chamber below, then quickly turn and pull up to the ledge on the right.

Drop down to the crack and then the ground, and walk through the barbwire.

The two areas that you backflip and spin to reach—while climbing the tall mesh wall—are each uniquely frustrating. Check the pictures. In the case of the upper jump to the Save Crystal, the trick is not to grab. Just do a straight jump and spin and you should make it to the ledge. To reach the Secret, the easy part is spinning and grabbing the ladder below the ledge. Getting up to the Secret is tricky. With Lara's hands on the ledge, drop and grab very quickly, so that Lara hangs from the ledge. Pull up before she has a chance to get her feet back on the ladder.

SECRET

Pull up to the wide spot in the crack and enter the dark area. There's a hole in the ceiling to use as an exit.

You have to jump around a corner to grab the edge of a slope and make it back up above the barbwire.

The button opens a nearby trapdoor. Climb to the hallway before you jump to the mesh and grab the Large Medi Pack.

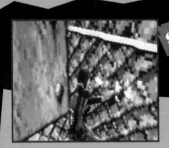

Climb the mesh to this point above the green grate, then jump and spin. Don't grab and you'll reach the ledge standing up.

SECRET

Backflip from the stripe in the red area, spin and grab the ladder. Climb up, then drop and grab very quickly so that Lara hangs from the ledge. From the hanging position, you can pull up to the ledge.

Climb up the mesh and crawl to the end of the passage. Grab the ammo and crawl back to where you can stand up.

Drop down into the room with the movable block and kill the guard. Expect more trouble when you open the door. Move the box to the opposite end of the track and the large area nearby is accessible.

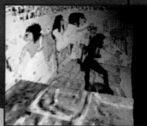

3

The first puzzle with an Egyptian motif is made harder **by the heights that Lara must negotiate.** The trick is to move the blocks before you even start jumping to ledges. Move the block in the control room, then the one in the high chamber, and then go back to the control room again. From there you can reach everything you need to make the high slope leading to the exit. On the highest ledges, stand and jump to the first small square, then run between the two squares where they form a corner with the wall.

In the large Egyptian area, climb to the opening in the ladder and follow the passage.

Move the box, then climb atop it to reach the exit. You actually have to jump and grab to reach the ledge.

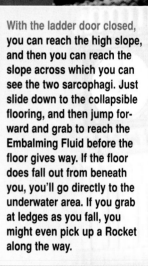

4

With the ladder door closed, you can reach the high slope, and then you can reach the slope across which you can see the two sarcophagi. Just slide down to the collapsible flooring, and then jump forward and grab to reach the Embalming Fluid before the floor gives way. If the floor does fall out from beneath you, you'll go directly to the underwater area. If you grab at ledges as you fall, you might even pick up a Rocket along the way.

Back in the large area, you can use the large pillar that has moved to reach a ledge high and to the left.

Slide down the red hallway and return to the room with the first block. Pull it to the central position.

Climb the tall pillar back in the large Egyptian room and spy a Switch on the wall to the left of the ladder.

Run, jump, and grab the short distance to get beneath the ledge. The Switch closes the ladder door.

Back closer to the floor, monkey-swing to two separate alcoves. The one opposite the Save Crystal has a Switch that opens a door high above.

Climb to the upper reaches of the room using the ladder. Jump the platforms to the left as you face the room.

Don't overlook the goodies nearby, and save your game at the top of the slope.

Slide, jump, and grab the walkway, then slide and do a standing jump forward and grab from the floor section that collapses beneath you. Take the Embalming Fluid and continue in that direction.

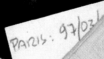

Crawling into the small room is painful, as the guard stands and caps you in the noggin until you can get to your feet and take action. Notice that, from the top of the sphinx, there are two routes: Down the back (the right way) and down the face (the silly way). If you do wind up on the face of the beast, you'll have to get creative to survive the fall. Try jumping sideways to land on the shoulder of the statue. If you slide backward and grab, you can usually live through it.

5

6

Dispose of the guard in the hallway and crawl through to the small room after checking your health.

Dispose of the guard and open the door to get the Rocket before continuing down to the large sphinx room.

Monkey-swing over to the far ledge and get the Save Crystal, then drop down to the head of the sphinx at the point where you get the wide angle.

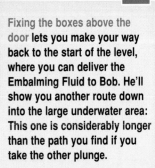

Fixing the boxes above the door lets you make your way back to the start of the level, where you can deliver the Embalming Fluid to Bob. He'll show you another route down into the large underwater area: This one is considerably longer than the path you find if you take the other plunge.

Look toward the rear of the sphinx and to the left. Walk to that corner and line up with the downward point of the ceiling. Hop backward, and then do a standing jump forward.

SECRET

You land on a ledge with a Small Medi Pack. Jump from there to the nearby pillar.

From the pillar run, jump, and grab the edge of the slope. Pull up, slide, and jump to the ledge where you can see the Save Crystal.

Down below, remove the hostility and gather ammo. The boxes above the doorway must be repositioned.

SECRET

By climbing to the ledge and then using the face of the first box to climb to an upper hallway, you can reconfigure the boxes and spy a Secret.

Jump and grab the edge of the blue ledge, and hang and drop to the floor to exit.

Moving the second box allows you to return to near the start of the level.

7

The UPV is a cool little toy, but it's kind of hard to aim as you pilot along. Use the small opening to draw the crocodiles in the area into a narrow space, and plink away at them as they come through the hole. There's one croc in attendance as you arrive, and another that shows up when you go for the Harpoons in the large chamber.

Use the Embalming Fluid at the ceremonial niche in the first room of the level. A passage opens nearby.

Swim down and grab the UPV. Bank to the right in the large chamber to spy an opening.

Head for the hole beneath the box as a crocodile pursues.

If you get inside the hole and pivot, you can easily shoot the croc as it comes through the narrow opening.

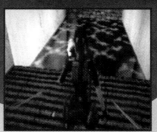

Gather the goodies from around the large area, returning to the small chamber to get air. Toward the far right corner of the room, a current sucks you to a new area.

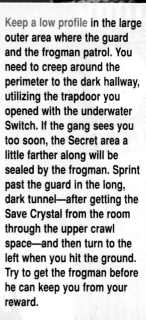

8

Keep a low profile in the large outer area where the guard and the frogman patrol. You need to creep around the perimeter to the dark hallway, utilizing the trapdoor you opened with the underwater Switch. If the gang sees you too soon, the Secret area a little farther along will be sealed by the frogman. Sprint past the guard in the long, dark tunnel—after getting the Save Crystal from the room through the upper crawl space—and then turn to the left when you hit the ground. Try to get the frogman before he can keep you from your reward.

Follow the underwater tunnel. Through the glass you can spy a Secret. Pull the lever on the wall to the right.

Up above, push the button to open another passage down in the tunnel.

Follow the underwater passage. When the area opens up, continue underwater to the right. You can surface in the area around another right turn. Below is a room with a Switch to pull.

SECRET

Near the room with the lever that opens the trapdoor, there's another small opening in the wall. Gather the stash.

Swim back past the underwater entrance to the large area, and continue down the narrow passage. On the right is a ledge. Climb out and keep low.

LONDON

There is no good substitute for experience in the large underwater area. Utilize the different lighting forms and the walls of the chambers to help lead you from Switch to Switch, mindful that they'll try to mess you up once in a while. Travel to every chamber to gather prizes, returning to the one small air pocket between trips. As you come into the large open area, the room with the air pocket is in the upper left-hand corner of the wall on the right. Realize that you're going to need every bit of air to get up the deep passages. On the return trip, don't even go looking for air in the room where you filled up previously: the pocket no longer exists.

After all that's come before, the home stretch of this level is a breeze. Everything is just as easy as it looks, though the boss confrontation against Sophia begins the next level.

SECRET

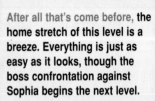

You have to stop the frogman from closing the Secret area beneath the water and to the right. There's also an underwater tunnel off this area.

In the large area, the object is to get air in the one small chamber and defend yourself while you gather the goodies. Switches in some of the chambers open doors with more Switches (See box 9).

Make sure you return to the air room before you try for each new Switch. You need the oxygen to make it safely.

Notice the walls surrounding this Switch don't look a lot like the outer chamber. Get familiar with the area or you'll be sucking in a lung-full of murky water.

The final Switch is a long haul. It opens the exit hatch—to the left of the air room—and also lets loose a flurry of frogmen.

Up the water passage, drop into the murk beneath the flaming ledges to find the lever that deactivates the trap. Why can't they all be that easy?

Dodge past the pistons and monkey-swing to the opening in the waterfall. Use the Boiler Room Key to open a hatch back through the large underwater chamber.

You don't get any chance to catch your breath en route to the second tall underwater chamber. Catch your breath, and stick to the left past the machinery.

Past the machinery and the guard, the hall dead-ends. Backtrack to discover a crawl space off the hall.

Follow the passages, running, jumping, and grabbing across the chasm until you reach the purple ledge. Time for a showdown.

London

THAMES WHARF

ALDWYCH

LUD'S GATE

CITY

SECRET

1 secret

The showdown with the evil Sophia is quick and dirty, **as the boss blasts you mercilessly while you attempt to get close to her. You** begin in the deserted office while Sophia has taken up a position across the street outside. As you attempt to negotiate the relatively pedestrian set of jumps and grabs, the boss rains down destructive bolts of energy. Try not to take any direct hits (famous last words). Wait for the boss to pause briefly for a recharge before you risk maximum exposure.

Lara arrives at the City showdown all alone because Sophia has left the office.

The pyrotechnics that begin as Lara nears the end of the hallway mean Sophia is fully charged.

The madwoman rains destruction down on the small landing. Head for the ramp.

Lara's main goal is not to get over to Sophia. **In fact, shooting her has no effect except** that maybe it gives the boss an easy target. Instead, Lara needs to climb to a small circuit box. Shooting the box electrocutes the boss in a truly impressive fashion.

Pull up top and turn around. There's a monkey swing overhead, but you don't need it.

You can run and jump the distance between the two ledges. It's much safer than swinging.

From the pillar where you grab after jumping, pull up above the monkey swing.

SECRET

Turn away from Sophia and look beyond the low box with the metal top.

Peering over the edge, you can perceive a Secret.

Hang on the ornate wall and spy an opening below.

Drop down and grab the ledge, then pull up to pilfer the goodies from the chamber.

LONDON

There's only one Secret in the level, **and it's worth picking up, if only for the brief respite Lara gains.** At the opposite end of the ledge where you drop down to the Secret, there's a button that opens a nearby trapdoor. Don't hesitate after you press that button. Roll and run back in the direction of the now-opened trapdoor or Lara gets blasted.

4

Keep one eye on Lara's health as you approach the level of the boss. **The less work Sophia has to do to aim, the more devastating her attacks.** At this range, there isn't much time to get out of the way. Suck it up. You've been hoarding those **Medi Packs,** anyway.

Hang and drop back to the floor outside, ready for an assault.

Sophia continues to hammer away as you climb back to the ledge with the small metal box.

Try not to get caught out in the open. Listen for the sound of your foe recharging her power.

In the opposite direction of the Secret is a walkway leading to a button.

Roll as soon as you push the button, as Sophia zeroes in for the kill.

Hustle back along the walkway.

A trapdoor has opened to the ledge above.

Pull up to the ledge. Now you're almost on the same level as the boss.

Now is not a good time to take in the view ...

Run along the upper walkway toward the ladder.

5

Take advantage of the small safe area near the base of the ladder. You have to be almost all the way back in the corner to avoid catching any flak, but it's worth a small wait for the boss to enter a recharge phase. At that point, you can climb the ladder without getting toasted the whole time.

You can hide out near the base of the ladder and wait for the boss to recharge.

Quickly climb up the ladder when the time is right.

At the top of the ladder, quickly crawl through the space on the right.

If you linger, or take too long scooping up the Small Medi Pack, you will pay.

Crawl through and then turn around and climb atop the crawl space.

6

Up above the crawl space, follow the walkway and run, jump, and grab the ledge. Drag your fried self over to the fuse box and give the boss her due. Memo to concerned maniacs: Those overly concerned with their own mortality should really try to avoid such high voltage.

Off to the right, you can see an easy jump to the bad side of town, but don't make that leap just yet.

Instead, run along the upper walkway.

Run, jump, and grab the distant ledge as the boss unloads to your right.

Climb up and keep moving straight ahead.

There's a fuse box on the wall. Hmmmm …

LONDON

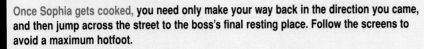

Once Sophia gets cooked, you need only make your way back in the direction you came, and then jump across the street to the boss's final resting place. Follow the screens to avoid a maximum hotfoot.

Shoot the fuse box and Sophia gets an overload of power.

You can see the last of the relics across the way, but the direct route is electrified.

Now's the time to head back and make that easy jump. It's on the other side of the crawl space.

If you played London as your last hub, the fourth and final relic is now in Lara's hands. It's time to go and put them to use. Next stop: Antarctica.

Run, jump, and grab the distant ledge to return to the area above the crawl space.

Stand at the very edge of the ledge and jump forward across the street.

You have to pick your way carefully through the charged area.

Climb the relatively tall wood-sided box.

Next, climb over the smaller box.

So close, and yet ... Climb over the box to the right of the artifact.

Press the button to cut the power; then take your prize.

London

Antarctica

ANTARCTICA

R.X.-TECH MINES

LOST CITY OF TINNOS

METEORITE CAVERN

SECRET
3
secrets

The first of the last levels is a tidy little adventure designed to let Lara get her feet wet—but hopefully not much more than that—in the colder clime. You'll notice that when Lara goes swimming in Antarctica, the numbing cold of the water immediately begins to sap her strength: a separate meter appears as a guide to show how long she can safely stay in the water. Not long at all, it turns out. Unless you're really hurting for ammo, it isn't worth risking Lara's life for a swim. She'll have to get in the water enough out of necessity. Look at it this way: At least you know that all that murky underwater stuff is behind you.

As the level begins, notice how the water saps Lara's health after a very short dunk. It almost makes the ammo nearby not worth the effort.

Follow the coastline past the hut. That's a Secret that you can't get at for some time.

Jump the channel alongside the ship.

The big ship is here for a purpose: To deliver the small Boat into Lara's tender care. Climb the cliffs and cross to the ship on the monkey swing. Be prepared to meet the area's stock enemy: the common thug. Nice jackets. Anyway, inside the ship is the mechanism for releasing the Boat from its perch at the back of the ship. Be mindful that you exit the ship to the rear, so that you can get the Secret accessible from that portion of the deck.

In the open area, you're going to have to get wet: climb quickly out at the low protrusion.

Jump in the water once more, and climb out near the front of the ship.

Climb the cliffs, and look for the monkey swing above to guide you in the right direction.

Swing to the end of the line and drop to the small ledge below.

The entrance on this end of the ship is through a hole in the deck. Check it out.

Down below, fight your way to the room with the machinery.

To the left of the machine is a Switch on the wall. It opens the trapdoor at Lara's feet.

ANTARCTICA

3

Once the Boat is dropped, **head back in the direction of the machinery room, but stop in the odd juncture to go through the hole in the ceiling. That's the way to the back of the ship.**

4

Once you collect the Secret from the cave off the ship's walkway, it's time to test out the Boat. It's pretty much a Cadillac compared to the Kayak and these are calm (if frigid) waters. Enjoy it a bit.

Drop down the trapdoor and follow the hallways, disposing of thugs along the way.

Look to the right in the odd-shaped juncture. There's also a hole in the ceiling on Lara's left.

In the direction of the orange pipe, whack the bad guy and drop through the trapdoor.

Down below, fight your way to the small window. Outside, you can see the Boat, the last of Lara's vehicles. Push the button and it falls to the water.

Double back and go up through the ceiling at the odd juncture.

Hang a right when you come out onto the deck and follow the walkway near the cliff.

SECRET

Jump and grab toward the opening from the edge of the deck and collect valuable prizes.

Bail from the ship to the waiting Boat below, confident that you can clamber aboard before dying.

Pilot the small craft around the ship, near the cliff, and down the waterway past the hut.

Pull over to the ledge a short way down the tunnel, and disembark.

5

When you stop to pick up the second Secret, **pop a Flare to see the interior of the crawl space better.** You can still slide, jump, and grab it OK whether you see it or not, but once inside you'll wish you had a Flare. At the monkey swing, you have to take it slow and steady so as not to fall off at the corners of the trick. At the end of the line, where the path splits in two, follow to the right and drop off from that end.

Slide, jump, and grab from the slope to catch a ledge above. You really need to use a Flare to see what's going on. Head to the right.

SECRET

Grab the Large Medi Pack, and backtrack through the crawl space. You'll drop down into the water near the Boat. Try for the ammo underwater ...

Guide the Boat farther along the tunnel, and it opens up into an area near a water gate. Hop ashore once more, and expect a welcoming committee.

Monkey-swing along the bars, careful at each turn. At the end of the line, the path divides: go to the end of the right-hand branch and drop.

Fight your way along the snowy tunnel. There are thugs and huskies in large numbers.

6

The tricky task of the big area is to open the fuel valves—properly—and then get power flowing to the nearby structures. Don't go messing with the valves. In the watery hole you can jump to the upper ledges, instead of into the water, but it really doesn't matter as long as you get out in a big hurry. Note that the water is shallow and harmless near the valves.

Past a raised structure, there's an opening in the side of a building. Proceeded with caution.

In the new area, press the button on the wall and loop around the building to the left.

Around the corner of the building there's a watery hole near a pipe. Drop to the water and swim quickly to the left to reach a ledge.

Check the fuel valves. The water here is only knee-deep, and not harmful.

Climb the ladder beyond the fuel valves to a new area.

PARIS: 97/03

ANTARCTICA

The layout of the area is relatively simple and inter-connected. **There are no unpleasant surprises along the paths except the occasional enemy. Keep those guns out and try to jump back for cover whenever an opportunity presents itself.** This can be a very Medi Pack-intensive stretch if you're soaking up all kinds of abuse.

7

8

Up top, the generator room is sealed.

Opposite the generator room, head around to the left in the outside area and follow the path.

The dogs are penned in for now, but you can come back and open the area when the power is flowing.

We thought we would never see the old slamming door trick, but all of a sudden here it is. Walk up to about one step in front of the doors and roll when they open wide. Ta-da! The bad guys upstairs, between you and the Crowbar, are a determined lot. When Lara first uses the Crowbar, she sets it at her feet in front of the opened door. Pick the Crowbar up again. You still have use for it.

Follow the path, wary of (non-lethal) pitfalls and heavy resistance.

You can climb down beneath the bridge to battle for ammo.

Back in the familiar area, by-pass the watery hole to the fuel valves and enter the large cave.

Defend yourself near the building.

The slamming doors are deadly almost on contact. But, as any good Tomb Raider knows, Lara can roll through them in a flash from about one step away.

Fight your way to the Crowbar upstairs. When you use it later on, don't just leave it lying there.

Head back to the familiar area via a new route, and back-track down the dark hallway.

9

Having regained the Crowbar, **stop by and properly configure the fuel valves as you saw in the diagram: as you enter, turn the second one on the left, and the farthest one as well. Head back to the generator room and get the juice flowing. That'll let you get at the Gate Key.**

Climb into the raised structure. Throw the Switch on the wall, and use the Crowbar to open the door.

Drop down the hatch and study the map. In order for the generator to power the surrounding area, valves two and four (the green ones) must be opened.

Head back to the generator room and throw the Switch to start the machinery.

Pop the pups and enter the building. All three buttons are now active.

Take the Gate Key from the desk. Time for the traditional big backtrack.

10

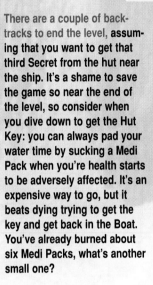

There are a couple of backtracks to end the level, **assuming that you want to get that third Secret from the hut near the ship.** It's a shame to save the game so near the end of the level, so consider when you dive down to get the Hut Key: you can always pad your water time by sucking a Medi Pack when you're health starts to be adversely affected. It's an expensive way to go, but it beats dying trying to get the key and get back in the Boat. You've already burned about six Medi Packs, what's another small one?

Head back to the metal monkey swing, near where you left the small Boat. In that building, the one which you open with the Crowbar, is the gate mechanism. Use the Gate Key and press the button.

Be ready for trouble when you prepare for departure.

Follow the waterway, making obvious stops to forage. At this landing, there's a small underwater alcove in front of the Boat and to the right. Inside is the Hut Key.

SECRET

If you take the Hut Key all the way back to the hut near the big ship, you'll find that a Save Crystal and some Flares are keeping company with a doggie.

If you continue to follow the waterway through the gate, you eventually exit and climb to a cabin. Fight your way around the structure, toward the door, and the level ends.

ANTARCTICA

Antarctica

SECRET
3
secrets

The R.X.-Tech Mines are almost transitional, setting Lara up for the big run through the Lost City just ahead. The frigid water here is designed to suck up a few of those Medi Packs, just as you really begin to need them. Try to be conservative, and realize that the flamethrowers won't torch you unless you go asking for it. There's plenty of things to shoot that are non-human, and more where that came from at Tinnos. The theme of this level is the Ore Carts, with which you travel around to a variety of areas in order to get a submersible operational. Be soft on the brakes, and also learn to duck down. On the second and third runs, there are low obstructions that pretty much knock Lara's block off if she isn't hunkered down.

To exit the seemingly dead-end hallway, run to the right through each successive gate. When you hear the double click, reverse direction to see an open passage.

Outside, a flamethrower roasts an experiment gone wrong.

You can decide whether the flamethrowers in these parts are friend or foe.

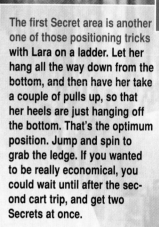

The first Secret area is another one of those positioning tricks with Lara on a ladder. Let her hang all the way down from the bottom, and then have her take a couple of pulls up, so that her heels are just hanging off the bottom. That's the optimum position. Jump and spin to grab the ledge. If you wanted to be really economical, you could wait until after the second cart trip, and get two Secrets at once.

In the large central chamber, three different Ore Carts are poised for a run.

Hit the lights in the control room, and slay the sub-human. Even as they die, they spew poison.

Climb atop the control room, and drop down to shimmy along its back ledge.

SECRET

At the ladder, lower Lara until she hangs by her hands, then pull her up so that her heels hang off the bottom of the ladder. Jump, spin and grab.

The small chamber behind the control room holds the level's first Secret stash.

The first Ore Cart you should ride is the one on the middle tier.

You'll want to lean and brake only slightly on the first run. Try to conserve some momentum as you head into the turn, as a jump is forthcoming.

The strange, almost wolfen monstrosities that roam the mines are an unwelcome addition to Lara's roster. To make matters worse, you're often forced to fight them with one eye looking over your shoulder, wondering how much room you have to the edge of some ledge. You need some big guns here. The Grenade or Rocket Launcher is not entirely out of the question. Try to start conserving Desert Eagle ammo with the final boss in mind.

Hit the track switch before the car comes to a stop, and survey the scene.

Duck below the drills, and circle to the left out back after exploring the crack in the far left wall.

A new manner of beast prowls this icy wilderness. Drop the mutant, then jump to the walkway below.

Hang and drop to the lower ledge.

Work the shimmies like switchbacks, moving all the way to one side before dropping down and reversing direction by grabbing a lower crack.

In the same area where you find the Crowbar on the metal ledge, don't overlook the hole high on the wall. There seems to be a distinctive shading to its underside: in reality, that's the ledge that you jump and shimmy across. To exit the area, you have to negotiate the tricky tops of the snow hills, angling for a barely visible opening a ways up the face of the cliff.

Pull up at the extreme lower left when you notice the ledge.

Be on guard as you traverse the tunnel.

In the wide-open area, gather the Crowbar from the metallic ledge.

Near the sub-human ambush, you can spy a small crawl space high on the wall. Watch your back!

From the rocks to the right of the opening, jump to the cliff and shimmy along the ledge. Throw the Switch inside.

ANTARCTICA

5

The huge smashing machines in the broad hallway aren't too big a threat, **as long as you time your sprint accordingly. It's OK to get nicked, just don't get flattened. Be sure to switch the Ore Cart track when you get back on the ride, or it's a real short trip.**

6

Using the Crowbar to get the Lead Acid Battery **is one half of the level's big puzzle solved. Now you only need the Winch Starter. Also, when you get back to the terminal, you can recheck the first Secret area. The Switch in that small room that you get to via the invisible shimmy opened up yet another Secret area inside. Explore the grounds thoroughly.**

To exit the area, you have to utilize the slopes, running and jumping up to a passage.

Head up the hallway, ducking down below the obstacles.

Dodge beneath the machines, and head up the slope.

At the top of the run, a sub-human waits to breathe in your face. Thanks so much.

Get back on the Ore Cart, and switch the car away from the dead end as you head back to the terminal.

Back at the terminal, use the Crowbar to pry open the door, and claim the Lead Acid Battery.

SECRET

If you return to the area of the first Secret, you'll see that another door has opened in the small area. Collect the goodies.

Now it's time for your second cart trip. Take the lowest track, and follow it to the left.

You'll need some serious speed to get across the chasm. Stay easy on the brake.

Develop your ducking ability, or Lara gets low-bridged to death.

In the area of the steamy walkway, the object is to lay hands on the Winch Starter, though they'll likely be cold hands. The Winch Starter is at the bottom of the relatively deep pool, so make sure you notice that only part of the ledge nearby is suitable for surfacing.

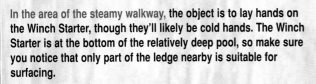

Follow the hallway where the cart stops. You'll take a long route back to the ride.

Rid the lower hallway of mutant beasts, and continue in the corridor.

Don't overlook the crawl space beneath the steamy walkway.

Crawl through the low area and drop into trouble.

Dispose of the freak and check the outside area. Specifically, look in the bottom of the pool.

The final Ore Cart ride is the one where ducking really becomes crucial. There's just no way to survive in the upright position, as those low barriers become almost commonplace. In order to lower the submersible pod, insert the battery and the Winch Starter—in the side and the back, respectively—and down goes the machine. Getting in without losing a bunch of health is a major accomplishment, and you should be ready to suck down a Medi Pack on your way back up through the long, tall tunnel. The slightest bump of a wall is going to cost you health near the top of the pool, and you don't want to go belly up with two hands on the ledge above.

You have to be quick to dive down and get the Winch Starter from the pool below the crane. The water is deadly cold.

Time for another wild ride: the upper Ore Cart calls.

Where the upper Ore Cart comes to a halt, a submersible pod is held by a crane.

Insert the battery in the side of the machine, and use the Winch Starter nearer the controls. The submersible pod submerges.

In the lowered position, you can swim down and into the pod, hopefully without taking too much damage.

ANTARCTICA

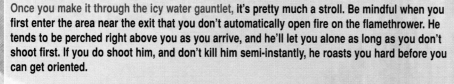

Once you make it through the icy water gauntlet, it's pretty much a stroll. Be mindful when you first enter the area near the exit that you don't automatically open fire on the flamethrower. He tends to be perched right above you as you arrive, and he'll let you alone as long as you don't shoot first. If you do shoot him, and don't kill him semi-instantly, he roasts you hard before you can get oriented.

From the pod, you need to reach another safe zone before heading for the surface.

The trip through the frigid water might have to be supplemented with Medi Packs.

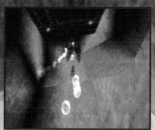
Swim down through the opening between the lights, and hook to the right.

The final little bit of puzzle is getting the final Secret of the level, lovingly placed within sight of the exit. There oughtta be a law. Watch your step in the chasm, of course, but there's nothing too tricky about the jumps. If you check out the scene from above, you may even see a way to bypass a bit of the jumping, simply by being brave from up above. That's not a guarantee, mind you, but Lara can take quite a drop as long as her health is good, and you are right near the end of the level.

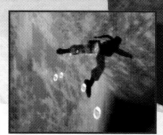
Be prepared to have Lara's health adversely affected, on the way up the tall tunnel, if not on the way down.

Up top, chat with the flamethrower.

Drop down to the ledge below the bridge.

Don't get caught staring into the chasm as freaks sneak from behind.

In the chasm, jump back and forth from ledge to ledge.

The final jump to the corner of the chasm ledges nets you the level's final Secret.

Backtrack to below the bridge, and jump up and grab. When you enter the small structure, the level ends.

Antarctica

SECRET

3 secrets

This is the big one. Sure, you'll go and fight the big boss next—maybe even go to All Hallows after that—but this level pulls out whatever stops are still in place, introducing tough, new monsters and puzzles, and also featuring one monster of a Secret: a timed run across a goodly portion of the level. Check the text blocks for more analysis, as there's quite a bit going on.

Welcome to the Lost City, found at last. Familiarize yourself with the immediate layout in peace.

Climb the ladder to the second story.

Throw the Switch to open a double door directly below. In you go.

The level pretty much cruises along for the first quarter or so. When you get tired of trying button combinations for the puzzle that lets you access the bridge, the correct sequence is to turn the first, second, and fifth Switches to the on position.

In a nook off the short hallway, lay claim to the Uli Key.

From the second floor, you can also jump to a central pillar. From there run, jump, and grab the ledge with the Save Crystal.

Use the Uli Key near the black grating in the courtyard and another section of the structure is accessible.

Drop onto the ledge outside the Switch-and-door combo, and spy another Switch.

Climb back up into the building from the Switch ledge, and cross the hallway to a sloped passage leading downward.

Throw the Switch down the sloped passage and the array of five Switches is yours to address. Turn the first, second, and fifth Switches on, as shown.

The Switches allow you to access an area near a monstrous busted bridge. Expect wasps of impressive girth as you collect the nearby Save Crystal.

ANTARCTICA

Sure, the wasps' nest is bad, but it's not near as nasty as the timed run. Just keep that in mind. Run and jump (no grab) from the top of the bridge and you can easily make the first platform. From the top of the other half of the bridge (en route to the second invisible platform) you can use both of the flat triangular sections. If you do that trick on the way back—hopping from one to the other instead of trying the longer jumps—realize that backfliping from one triangle section to another is safer than the forward jump. The large, magical monsters are serious trouble, but not resistant to a grenade or three.

3

4

Climb the ledges near the Save Crystal cave and jump to the top of the bridge across the chasm. Before you drop down, punish the wasps and share their Secret.

SECRET

High above the surface of the broken bridge, invisible platforms guide you toward the nest.

From the closest unseen platform, you can run, jump, and grab to the opening of the nest. Don't fall in the hole.

The big closed room where you duke it out with three of the king freaks in rapid succession is a stern test. You need to be pretty aggressive, perhaps hauling out some heavy artillery to help even the odds. When the battle's won, look down the short hallway off the room and throw the Switch. That opens a walkway on a high ledge in the outer area. That walkway leads to the huge room of ledges and Switches, and, eventually, to that big Secret. Begin in the big room by working your way along the wall to the left and throwing the Switch in the upper alcove opposite where you came into the room. After throwing the first Switch, jump off to the left and squeeze through another crawl space to discover a second Switch. From there, you need to use the new configuration of the ledges to make it to the floor with minimal wear and tear. Angle for the pillars concentrated in one area below.

Backtrack across the invisible platforms and dropdown across the break in the bridge. Follow the tunnel to the right after grabbing the Small Medi Pack on the left.

Defend yourself against the monsters as you enter their territory. Hop side to side to get in some licks before they close the distance.

Pass by the lovely swinging bowls of coals. If one touches you in the slightest, combustion occurs.

In the next area, duck under the ledge to the left to draw the wasps down into range. Head in that direction.

Down the hallway, hit the Switch and battle the three big, magical monsters that appear in short order. At least there's room to move in the chamber.

A Switch down a short hallway from the major monster battle room opens a crawl space in the outside area. Use the pillar near the gate and duck the traps en route to a large new area.

In the large chamber, Lara must change the height of certain platforms by manipulating the many Switches.

Once you throw the floor-level Switch in the large room, **climb to the ledge that raises high above.** There's another Switch to throw, and another ledge to visit. Ultimately, you want see a small platform beneath the walkway near the room's entrance. If you step back from the edge of the platform above and jump forward as if purposely trying to jump short of the walkway, you should be able to hit the platform below. Monkey-swing along the underside of the walkway and throw the Switch down there to open the exit.

Drop to the walkway and head to the left along the wall. The Switch to the right is a timed Switch leading to a Secret. You need to open the exit to the room before throwing it.

One of the final keys to manipulating the Switches and ledges properly is to realize that you can monkey-swing along the underside of the walkway (See box 5).

The run for the timed Secret is tough. **Keep sprinting the whole while**—except maybe when negotiating the swinging urns—and don't even try to hop carefully down to the level of the door. Watch your health—and certainly be careful with several landings in order to keep your health out of the lethal range. However, getting down to the door is hard enough without having to do it stylishly.

When you succeed in opening the exit to the large chamber, it's time to test the Secret Switch. Save your game first.

Throw the Switch and run back down the hallway. Off the walkway on the left is a ledge you can drop to. Hang and drop from there to the floor.

Throw the Switch in the hallway and hustle through to the room with the pillar of light.

Hook to the right of the light and head up the stairs. Continue into the narrow hallway.

Down the hallway, hang a left back through the bowls of coals. Lovely.

Cross the bridge and bail off the right side near the cliff face. Don't stop to think, just rumble down the slopes and pillars to the bottom of the gorge.

SECRET

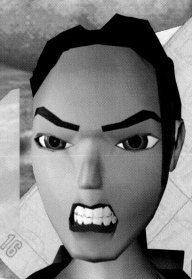

If you lose any significant time en route, the door down here will be closed. If you do make it inside, throw the Switch twice to exit.

Up above the pillar of light room are the four tests of the elements that will net Lara four Oceanic Masks. Those masks work in the statues below to take Lara to the big boss.

ANTARCTICA

The Earth puzzle is probably the easiest of the four, since the route is direct and you can avoid a lot of falling rock simply by walking. In order to get the Secret back in the area near the pillar of light room, you need to jump up the low ledges near where you see the icon. On the way back, you need to make a couple of tricky jumps in order to avoid taking the big plunge because the cavern has exploded into dangerous portions. When you jump across the narrow section of quicksand to the small triangle section, do so with good health: there's a ton of rocks with Lara's name on 'em headed her way. As in all cases, when you make it back to the finishing hallway, approach the dark gate. It'll open automatically, and you'll be back near the light pillar.

In the Earth area, you encounter a thick mire. Head around to the right and keep plowing forward along that wall.

Exit the quicksand to the right, past the rune on the wall. You have to hop some of these nearby low ledges so that you can get a Secret later on (See box 7).

The Oceanic Mask waits up the walkway and out of the muck. When you take the prize, the roof begins to fall, and the landscape becomes much less friendly (See box 7).

Walk patiently out of the area. There are some risky jumps ahead, so you don't need to get whacked by boulders en route.

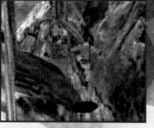

The worst of the exit jumps is around a tight corner to a slanted ledge. Stick the landing.

If you threw the Switch in the Earth puzzle area, you can now climb atop a large block near the bowls of coals. Time your run carefully.

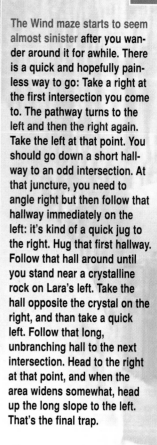

The Wind maze starts to seem almost sinister after you wander around it for awhile. There is a quick and hopefully painless way to go: Take a right at the first intersection you come to. The pathway turns to the left and then the right again. Take the left at that point. You should go down a short hallway to an odd intersection. At that juncture, you need to angle right but then follow that hallway immediately on the left: it's kind of a quick jug to the right. Hug that first hallway. Follow that hall around until you stand near a crystalline rock on Lara's left. Take the hall opposite the crystal on the right, and than take a quick left. Follow that long, unbranching hall to the next intersection. Head to the right at that point, and when the area widens somewhat, head up the long slope to the left. That's the final trap.

The Wind area is a merciless maze of strangely intersecting corridors.

Head to the right at this juncture.

Once more, head to the right and follow the long hallway.

Jump back and forth from ledge to ledge to induce the spiked logs to roll down. At the top of the trap is another of the Oceanic Masks.

The water puzzle is complicated by deadly underwater blades that serve to chip away at Lara's health as she explores. Realize it's much better to be going with a blade, not against it, when you're trying to sneak past. Follow the blade as it passes the opening and slip through behind it instead of cutting in front of it at any old angle. Drop through the initial blades to the area of the strange underwater clock. The alcove you need is the left-hand one, where you can throw a Switch and get some air. After pulling the lever, swim out of the small room and in through the opening on the right-hand side of the clock face. Swim up to a new area. In the new area, there's air up above and an open door with a Switch for you to pull. Pull the Switch, and the doorway in the opposite blade base opens. Grab the Oceanic Mask and throw the Switch. Get some air and return to the clock room via the crevice near the first Switch. Back in the clock room, grab a breath and then head through the hole at the bottom of the clock. You should get sucked to a shallow tunnel. Follow the path.

The clock-like piece is the center of the underwater puzzle (See box 9).

Do you suppose there's going to be some marathon swims? (See box 9).

The long swim sessions end in a shallow tunnel. It's about time, by then.

The fire puzzles are high on drama, but not too tough. You'll see a map to the area if you stand on the block near the entrance.

Use the map to help you pick your way through the hot spots.

The dragon heads are puffing on invisible platforms. You need to move quickly across them to keep from getting singed (See box 10).

Hanging from the sides of the platforms is safe, though you need to be quick and have good timing to pull up and get to the next block.

Jump off to the right to throw the Switch.

When you place all four masks, you need only get the second Uli Key from the denizens of the pool room.

The Uli Key sits on a ledge off the larger pool room. Use it on the lock in the hall near the pillar of light, and then Lara can jump down to the Meteorite Cavern.

The final elemental puzzle—and these really could be taken in any order, obviously—is getting across a collection of flaming pillars, and then getting past some dragon heads bellowing flame onto invisible platforms. If you stand on the big block near the entrance to the flame pillars, you can see a map of the pillars above Lara's head. It may take a bit to get oriented, but once you see what's going on it's pretty much a cruise. Just as a precaution, don't linger on any platform for very long. In the case of the dragon heads, run and jump to the first block, then stand and jump to the third. From there, step off, grab the ledge, and get your timing together. Move to the right-hand side of the block. You'll want to pull up and pivot to the right to jump to the ledge with the Switch. The Oceanic Mask is in the room off of the nearby ledge. When you have all four of the masks, slap those suckers in a pillar; any of the four pillars accept any mask. Go get the Uli Key and put that in the lock in the short hallway nearby. The Uli Key (number two) is in that room full of small pools—the one you sprinted through en route to the timed Secret.

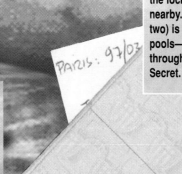

PARIS: 97/03

16

ANTARCTICA

Antarctica

ANTARCTICA

R.X.-TECH MINES

LOST CITY OF TINNOS

METEORITE CAVERN

SECRET
0
secrets

1

The showdown is at hand in the Meteorite Cavern. The boss is big and spidery. Lara is smart, and hopefully, heavily armed. The boss has one big trick: a tremendous burst of evil energy that can't be avoided, and is always lethal. Sound like fun? What's a girl to do …

2

The catch is that the big boss won't fire his death ray **as long as the meteorite—the hole in the middle of the cavern, in essence—is between him and Lara. With that in mind, Lara need only keep her distance and plink away.**

The big boss is one mean, king freak.

The area you have to fight in isn't very hospitable either.

If you're lucky, the boss will only try and shove you to an inglorious demise.

If the boss gets off one shot, Lara is toast.

Sprint the straightaways and slow through the turns. You should be able to keep your distance.

Unless the pit is in between Lara and the boss …

… the lady gets lit.

Sprinting through the tuns is risky, as the slopes of the outer edge are an invitation to disaster.

If the boss has you in his sights, you might as well unload some ammo: maybe you can stun him before he takes the shot.

Occasionally, the boss will offer only a love bite. Rarely. Closing the gap is not advised.

3

Of course, to bring the boss down a notch and make him ripe for destruction, Lara must also gather up the four fragments of the meteor rock (the relics) from the alcoves around the room. In order to do that without the boss unloading, she has to stun him. Choose a decent weapon—preferably the Desert Eagle, as it has a rapid rate of fire to go with its wallop. Five of the ten shots with the Desert Eagle will stun the boss. You can only get off five at a time before he gets uncomfortably close, but open up the gap and deliver five more and the boss drops. Momentarily.

Ideally, you want to fire the first salvo of your attack as the boss passes in front of an alcove where you have yet to claim the artifact.

When the boss crumples, it's time to grab an artifact.

4

Hustle to the closest alcove, as long as there's still an artifact there and you're not actually going toward the boss.

You've only got a few seconds to sprint into the alcove, snatch up the prize, and get back to a position across the hole from the boss.

Even if the boss sits stunned, you have to make sure that he's across the pit and in a direct line.

Your positioning must be very good before it's safe to try for a relic. Ideally, the boss is directly across the chamber, and the relic is directly behind you. Of course, it seldom works out that way, so you have to consider that the boss will wake up about the time you return to the walkway from the relic alcove. Will he be able to shoot you right away, or will you be able to break off to one side. Also make sure that a safe amount of space is between you two. It's hard to resist making a run when the boss goes down, but realize that if he falls right beside you, you can't head for the nearest alcove. Just not gonna happen.

If he comes to and has a clear line of fire, he can strike anywhere.

The boss almost always circles from Lara's right to her left, so you'll want to break to the right when coming back from an alcove.

Keep stunning and running until you collect all four of the artifacts.

When the last of the four relics is in Lara's possession, the meteor sinks from the ceiling to the central pool. The boss is now vulnerable.

Bring that bad boy down.

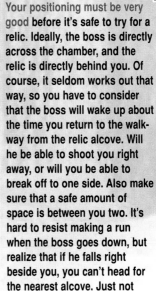

ANTARCTICA

When the boss goes boom, **you still have a little work to do. Ain't that always the way.** You need to climb up out of the cavern and make your escape.

The backflip to the statue's hand **is the trickiest part. You did save your game, didn't you?**

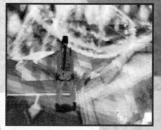

The boss goes out with a bang.

After the fireworks ... silence.

Say, is that a ladder?

Climb the ladder to the very top.

Continue past the face into the highest corner, than back down one notch.

Right about there ...

Backflip to the hand of one of the huge statues.

Jump from there to the central ledge.

Follow the tunnel off to the left.

You emerge high above the cavern. Monkey-swing to a central large ledge.

In the upper area, **a few stragglers still haven't learned the error of their ways. School them.**

From the ledge, jump to the central rocky platform.

Take one last look ...

Through the fence, **follow the sounds of chopper blades to the rendezvous. Game over?**

Climb up the rocks.

A fresh snow is falling.

Slide down the slope and turn to the right.

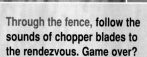

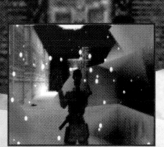

Dispose of any lingering rabble.

Push the button on the wall.

Go through the open gate. You can hear your escape route ...

The helicopter swoops in low.

Go through the gate toward the helicopter for the finishing cut scene.

Antarctica

ANTARCTICA

All Hollows

SECRET

0 secrets

The tidy little trip to All Hallows is your reward for finding all of the Secrets in the game. If you notched them all, you can save your game when the Meteorite Cavern is behind you and load up All Hallows from there. Though there are several cool things to do, this is just for grins. There are only two enemies at the very end, and Lara's cupboard is bare (check the inventory). Be sure not to lose any health at all before you crash through cathedral dome. Lara needs full health to survive the plunge.

There is a tricky area at the very beginning of the level. In order to reach this area, Lara must do a twist jump in midair on the very first slide into the area and grab hold of the ledge at the end. From here she can drop and grab a lower ledge and shimmy left until she can pull herself up into the pickup area.

1

Climb the metallic ledges.

Make your way around the ledges toward the central construct.

Run and jump up the slope to the ledge with some Flares.

2

Gather the Flares from the ledge, then monkey-swing over and drop into the cathedral. Now where did you put that Cathedral Key?

3

Follow along with the screens if you're into expedience. After all the Tomb Raiding you've done to get here, this is a stroll.

Jump from the Flares to the central platform.

Monkey-swing about a meter and drop. Lara crashes through the cathedral ceiling.

Lara just barely survives the fall if she has full health. Luckily, there's a Large Medi Pack on the landing.

4

Make your way around the ledges, moving from one new area to the next. All Hallows is a straightforward trip.

Collect the Flares from the purplish platform and head around the room to the walkway above the bookshelf.

Up above the bookcase is an alcove with a Switch. Throw it.

Use the small section to hang and drop down to floor level.

Climb up here.

5

The relatively low heights in All Hallows seem a bit pedestrian, once you've been to Mudubu Gorge …

Jump to the central structure.

Run, jump, and grab, and then shimmy left.

6

The drop from the rope slider is tricky. Just as you enter the light—perhaps an instant later—you need to drop if you intend to hit the ledge below. Considering the alternatives, try for the ledge.

Throw the Switch in the upper alcove and a dim hallway opens at ground level.

Run across the collapsing flooring. Throw the Switch at the end of the hall.

Monkey-swing above the spikes back to the main room.

Jump from the ledge above the bookcases to the monkey swing. Head to the left.

Drop and grab from the end of the monkey swing, and pull up into the small area.

Climb up past the rope slider.

Collect the Vault Key.

When Lara hits the lights, it's about time to let go. Too soon or not soon enough and it's spike city.

ALL HOLLOWS

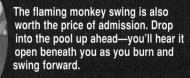

7

The flaming monkey swing is also worth the price of admission. Drop into the pool up ahead—you'll hear it open beneath you as you burn and swing forward.

8

Go down the trapdoor. Lara gets in a little target practice before she gets some R&R. When you go for the goodies, the level ends.

From the ledge where Lara lands, grab the nearby pillar and pull up into the small space.

Hang off the other side of the pillar, and a door opens.

Lara will take a flaming monkey swing ...

Just be sure to drop off into the saving pool of water.

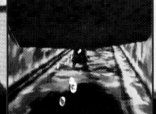

Time your swim past the piston.

Push the button. On the upper ledge to the right as you face the button is a Small Medi Pack.

Up above the ladder, roll and grab the ledge to defeat the trapdoor. Jump forward over the gap.

The trapdoor that opened is very near where you exit to the outside area.

Open the vault and shoot through the two gratings nearby. Drop into the water hole in the vault.

Surface to find a guard and his dog: the level's only two kills. When you explore the area, the level ends.

Only Eidos challenges your imagination!

OMIKRON *The Nomad Soul*

THE UNHOLY WAR — OUT THINK. OUT MANEUVER. OUT LIVE.

TOMB RAIDER III — ADVENTURES OF LARA CROFT

FIGHTING FORCE 64

PlayStation

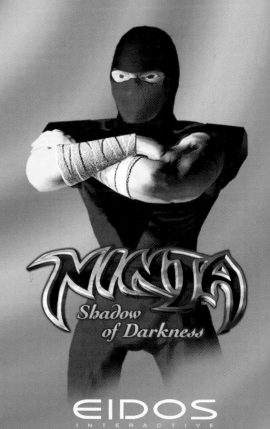

NINJA *Shadow of Darkness*

www.eidosinteractive.com

EIDOS INTERACTIVE

The Unholy War and the related characters are trademarks of Crystal Dynamics. © 1998 Crystal Dynamics. All rights reserved. Tomb Raider III, Lara Croft, Ninja: Shadow of Darkness and Fighting Force and trademarks of Core Design. © 1998 Core. Eidos Interactive and Omikron are trademarks of Eidos, Plc. © 1998 Eidos. All rights reserved. PlayStation and the PlayStation logos are registered trademarks of Sony Computer Entertainment Inc.

Check out these other hot titles in the Eidos Strategy Line-up!

BRAVEHEART
EIDOS
Coming March 1999
3Dfx

WARZONE 2100
EIDOS
Coming February 1999
3Dfx

COMMANDOS
BEHIND ENEMY LINES
EIDOS
OUT NOW!

EIDOS
INTERACTIVE

www.eidosinteractive.com

Braveheart TM & © 1999 Paramount Pictures and 20th Century Fox Corporation. Commandos: Behind Enemy Lines and Eidos Interactive are trademarks of EIDOS plc. © 1997-1998 Eidos. All rights reserved.